PICTURE YOURSELF
Learning
Microsoft® Access™ 2007

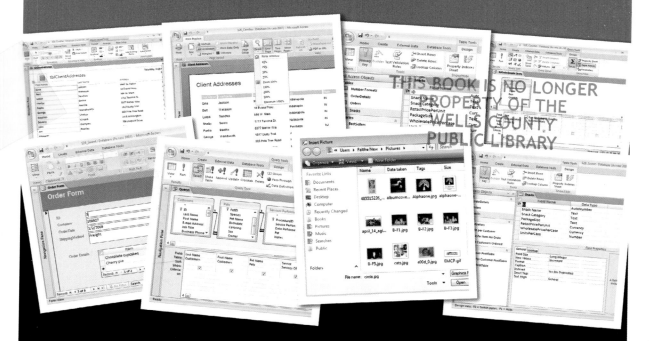

D1088546

Faithe Wempen

COURSE TECHNOLOGY
CENGAGE Learning™

**Picture Yourself Learning
Microsoft Access 2007
Faithe Wempen**

**Publisher and General Manager,
Course Technology PTR:** Stacy L. Hiquet

Associate Director of Marketing:
Sarah Panella

Manager of Editorial Services:
Heather Talbot

Marketing Manager:
Jordan Casey

Acquisitions Editor:
Megan Belanger

Project Editor and Copy Editor:
Kim Benbow

Technical Reviewer:
Lisa Bucki

PTR Editorial Services Coordinator:
Jen Blaney

Interior Layout:
Shawn Morningstar

Cover Designer:
Mike Tanamachi

Indexer:
Sharon Shock

Proofreader:
Brad Crawford

Microsoft, Access, Windows, and Internet Explorer are either registered trademarks or trademarks of Microsoft Corporation in the United States and/or other countries. All other trademarks are the property of their respective owners.

Library of Congress Control Number: 2008934343
ISBN-13: 978-1-59863-841-7
ISBN-10: 1-59863-841-6

Course Technology
25 Thomson Place
Boston, MA 02210
USA

Cengage Learning is a leading provider of customized learning solutions with office locations around the globe, including Singapore, the United Kingdom, Australia, Mexico, Brazil, and Japan. Locate your local office at:
international.cengage.com/region

Cengage Learning products are represented in Canada by Nelson Education, Ltd.

For your lifelong learning solutions, visit **courseptr.com**
Visit our corporate website at **cengage.com**

Printed in the United States of America
1 2 3 4 5 6 7 11 10 09

To Margaret

Acknowledgments

THANK YOU TO THE WONDERFUL STAFF AT Cengage Learning for another job well done. Thanks to my editors Megan Belanger, Kim Benbow, and Lisa Bucki, as well as the production department staff, who so seldom get the recognition they deserve.

About the Author

FAITHE WEMPEN is a teacher and internationally known expert in Microsoft Office, PC hardware, and A+ certification preparation, with over 100 technical books to her credit, as well as college textbooks, magazine articles, and Web site content. She has educated over a quarter of a million online students for corporate clients, including Sony, CNET, and Hewlett-Packard, and is an adjunct professor of Computer Information Technology at Purdue University.

Table of Contents

Introduction—Welcome to Access 2007!

THIS PICTURE YOURSELF GUIDE from Course Technology/Cengage Learning will help you master Microsoft Access, the database component of the Microsoft Office 2007 suite of applications. You'll learn how to create your own databases, including tables, queries, forms, and reports, and how to share them with others.

The *Picture Yourself* guides use a visual approach with illustrations of what you will see on your screen linked with instructions for the mouse movements or keyboard operations to complete your task. Computer terms and phrases are clearly explained in non-technical language, and expert tips and shortcuts help you produce professional-quality work.

Who This Book Is For

This book is for people who are new to Microsoft Access, but not necessarily new to Office applications in general. Access is usually not the first Office application someone picks up because it is more of a development tool than a clerical one. So this book assumes that you can use a mouse, start applications, and manage files (such as performing Save, Open, and Print operations).

This book does not assume any previous understanding of databases in general, though, or of Access specifically. Along the way, you will learn some terminology basics that will serve you well as you work with other database applications, too.

How to Use This Book

Just jump right in! If you are new to Access, start with Chapter 1; if you already have an existing Access database, skip to the chapter that pertains to your interest.

Creating a
Database

PICTURE YOURSELF SEARCHING your collection of audio CDs, trying to remember who sang a certain song that you want to play for a friend. You fumble through dozens of CD cases, scanning for the song title, but to no avail. Now picture looking up the song title in a database you've created of your CD collection, and quickly and easily determining which artist and CD to pull from the shelf.

Access is a very popular database management program for personal computers. It creates small- and medium-sized databases that consist of one or more data tables plus helper objects like queries, forms, and report layouts. In this chapter, you will learn some basic database terminology, and you'll see how Access is organized and how to use it to create a new database with a simple table in it.

Getting Started with Access

A DATABASE IS A STRUCTURED collection of data. Your address book is a database, for example, and so is the local telephone directory. Retail stores, both on the Internet and in a brick-and-mortar store, maintain large databases of products for sale, and nearly all businesses have databases of their customers and their orders and purchases.

A database can consist of one or more tables. A **table** is a two-dimensional row-and-column grid, like a spreadsheet. A table's structure is defined by its fields. A **field** is a name that represents a category of information, such as FirstName or City. In an address book, for example, the fields might be FirstName, LastName, Address, City, State, and ZIP. Fields can have different types. A text field can hold any combination of alphabetic characters, symbols, and digits. A number field can contain only numbers.

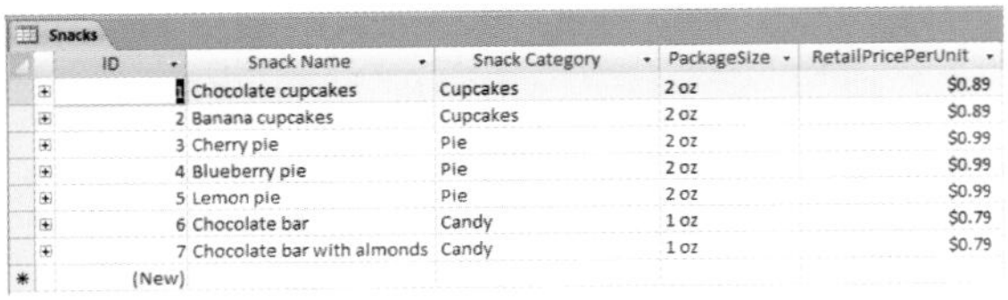

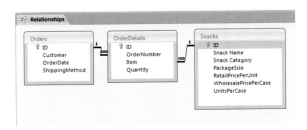

Figure 1-1
An Access table shown in Datasheet view

The data stored in the table is organized by **records**. Each record contains the information for one instance (all fields). For example, a record in an address book might consist of the entries in all the fields for one particular person: John Doe, 123 East Main Street, Macon, IL, 62544.

In Access, the default view of a table is **Datasheet view**, which shows the records and fields in a spreadsheet-like format (see Figure 1-1).

Access can create **relational databases**—that is, databases that consist of multiple tables with links between them. For example, a business may have a Customers table for storing customer contact information and an Orders table for storing information about orders placed. Each customer in the Customers table has a unique ID, and each order in the Orders table references a specific customer by his or her ID number. You can manage these relationships in Access in a special view called **Relationships**, as shown in Figure 1-2.

Figure 1-2
The Relationships view of the database shows the fields from each table and how they are related.

Understanding Access Objects

Data is stored only in tables in an Access database. There are many other types of objects that can exist in an Access database, however, to support you in managing and using that data.

Queries are alternative views of a table that enable you to filter out unneeded fields and/or records, and sort records in ascending or descending order by a particular field. You can also use a query design to combine fields from multiple tables into a single datasheet. Query results appear in Datasheet view, the same as tables.

Data can be entered into tables from the Datasheet view, but inexperienced users may find it a bit intimidating to do so. The alternative is to create a user-friendly **form** for data entry and editing, showing only one record at a time, as in Figure 1-3.

Figure 1-3
A form makes it easier to enter data into a table.

You can print a datasheet as it appears onscreen, but the layout may not be very attractive. As an alternative, you can create **report** layouts, which present the data from a table or query in an attractive format. A report can include specific fonts, sizes, and colors for text, as well as logo graphics. See Figure 1-4.

Top 10 Biggest Orders

#	Invoice #	Order Date	Company	Sales Amount
1	41	3/24/2006	Hart Parts	$13,800
2	38	3/10/2006	The ACME Corporation	$13,800
3	47	4/8/2006	Colvin Enterprises	$4,200
4	46	4/5/2006	Accessibility Plus	$3,690
5	58	4/22/2006	ACME Corporation	$3,520
6	79	6/23/2006	Colvin Enterprises	$2,490
7	77	6/5/2006	Z-Axis Learning	$2,250
8	36	2/23/2006	Beachwarez	$1,834
9	78	6/5/2006	ACME Corporation	$1,560
10	44	3/24/2006	ACME Corporation	$1,511

Figure 1-4
A report presents data in an attractive printable format.

There are several other types of less-common objects used in some databases, including macros, modules, and data access pages. These types are not covered in this book.

Creating a New Database

You will create a new database file whenever you start work for a new company or project. A single database file holds all the tables, queries, reports, and other objects needed for that company or project. You can then reopen that database file whenever you want to work on it.

When you open Access, the Getting Started with Microsoft Office Access screen appears. At the left is a selection of templates; at the right is a selection of recently opened database files. In the center is a Blank Database button and some links to additional templates and information online about Access. See Figure 1-5.

Figure 1-5
The Getting Started screen appears when you open Access.

The following steps show you how to create a new, blank database file, which you will need to follow along with the rest of this part of the book.

1. From the Getting Started window, click the Blank Database icon. A Blank Database section appears in the lower-right panel, shown in Figure 1-6. (You can redisplay the Getting Started window at any time by choosing Office > New.)

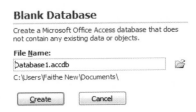

Figure 1-6
Enter the file name and location to create the new blank database file.

2. Type the file name you want in the File Name text box.

3. The default location appears below the text box. If you want to change that, click the folder button to the right of the text box, browse for a different location, and click OK.

4. Click Create. The new database file is created.

Understanding the Access Interface

After you create a new database (or open an existing one), the main part of the Access interface becomes available, and a new table appears in Datasheet view. As with other Office 2007 applications, the main feature of the Access interface is the tabbed **Ribbon** across the top.

The **Navigation pane** also appears, on the left side of the screen. It lists all the objects in the database. In Figure 1-7, there is only one object, the new table that Access has automatically started. It does not yet have a real name, so it is referred to as Table1.

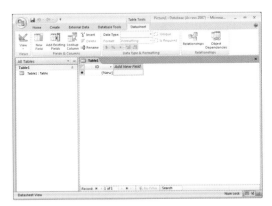

Figure 1-7
The Access interface

You can open and close the Navigation pane as needed. To close it from its open state, as in Figure 1-7, click the << button at its top. When it is closed, as in Figure 1-8, click the vertical words "Navigation Pane" or click the >> button.

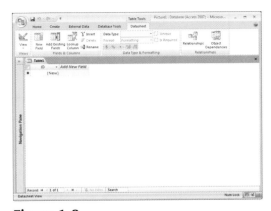

Figure 1-8
The Navigation pane is hidden.

Creating a Table in Datasheet View

TABLES ARE THE BASIS OF any database. The tables hold the data records that you will enter. Although you can make changes to a table's design after you have begun entering records into it, some rework is usually required to fill in the values for any added fields and to ensure that existing data matches any new rules you impose for the content. Therefore, it is a much better idea to finalize table structure *before* entering any data into the table.

Chapter 2 covers another way of creating a table: using Design view. Design view is the choice of most database professionals because of the extra options it offers, but it is somewhat more complex, too. That's why it needs its own chapter.

You can create the fields here in Datasheet view if you like. Double-click the Add New Field text at the top of the next available column, and type a field name (see Figure 1-9). Repeat that for each field you want to create.

Figure 1-9
Create field names by double-clicking a column heading and typing them.

You can create a new table in Datasheet view any time, not just when you initially create the database. To start a new table in Datasheet view, choose Create > Tables > Table.

Adding Fields to a Datasheet

When you start a new database, as you just saw, Access starts a new table for you automatically and opens it in Datasheet view. By default it has only one field, called ID, which is an AutoNumber type field. In other words, you do not enter values into it; Access automatically enters a unique value in that field for each record you create.

Renaming a Field

To rename a field, click the field's column heading and then choose Datasheet > Fields & Columns > Rename. Type the new name, and press Enter.

Inserting or Deleting a Field

Generally speaking, you should create the fields in the order you want them to appear in the table. If you make a mistake and need to insert a new field between two existing ones, you can do so.

Click the column that the new one should appear to the left of, and choose Datasheet > Fields & Columns > Insert. Alternatively, you can right-click an existing field (any cell in its column) and click Insert Column.

To delete a field, select the field (by clicking its column heading), and then do either of the following:

> ▶ **Choose Datasheet > Fields & Columns > Delete.**

> ▶ **Right-click the field and click Delete Column.**

If the field you are deleting contains data, a warning message appears; click Yes. You cannot undo field deletions.

Saving the Table Structure and Closing a Table

When you are finished with the table, close its datasheet by right-clicking the tab and choosing Close. If you have made changes to the table's structure (which you have!), a dialog box appears asking whether you want to save changes to it.

Click Yes, and a Save As dialog box opens. In it, type the name you want to assign to the table, and click OK. See Figure 1-10.

Figure 1-10
Saving a table

Some database designers make it a policy to assign prefixes to object names that reflect the object type so they can more easily keep track of the type. For example, they precede all table names with tbl, so an employees table might be called tblEmployees, and a query based on that table might be called qryEmployees. It is up to you whether you want to use a naming convention, and if so, what prefixes you want to use.

Using a Table Template

In Chapter 2, you will learn how to set up properties and types for fields that will help them store your data more precisely, such as limiting the number of characters that the field will accept, setting a field type that limits the entries to certain types of characters, and more. You will set up each field manually with the exact properties that are appropriate for the data it will contain.

Access offers a shortcut, though, for all that manual field setup. You can use a **table template** that contains all the fields you will need for a certain purpose, including all the types and properties that you would normally have to configure yourself. Access 2007 offers table templates for the following tables: Contacts, Tasks, Issues, Events, and Assets. You can then delete any fields that you don't want, and/or modify any field properties as needed. (See Chapter 2 for details.)

To create a new table with a table template, choose Create > Tables > Table Templates, and then click the desired template on the menu that appears. See Figure 1-11. The new table appears in Datasheet view, with all the fields set up.

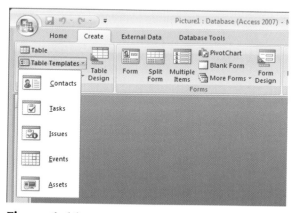

Figure 1-11
Create a table based on a template.

Using a Field Template

Even if none of the table templates contains anything close to the fields you want, there is still some help available. You can pick and choose the individual fields from any of the table templates by using **field templates**. Access allows you to individually insert any of the fields from any of the templates into an existing table. There are also some generic field templates for certain field types, such as number, currency, date/time, and hyperlink.

To use a field template to insert a new field:

1. From Datasheet view, choose Datasheet > Fields & Columns > New Field. The Field Templates task pane appears at the right.

2. Collapse/expand the lists of fields in the task pane to find the field you want to insert.

3. Drag the field name from the task pane to the datasheet. When the mouse pointer is in a position where you can drop the field, it turns into a white pointer with a plus sign on it, and an orange vertical line appears to show where the field will be inserted. See Figure 1-12. Alternatively, you can quickly add the field to the far-right position in the table by double-clicking the field name.

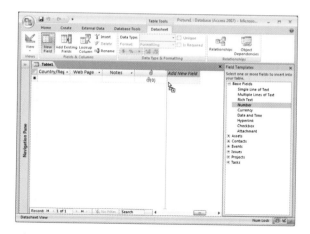

Figure 1-12
Add template fields to a table.

When you are finished with the field templates, click the Close (X) button in the upper-right corner of the Field Templates task pane to close it, or choose Datasheet > Fields & Columns > New Field again to turn it off.

Copying a Table

If you need two or more tables that are very similar in structure, you might want to copy an existing table. You can make a copy of only the structure of the table, or you can copy both the structure and the data records (if it contains any data records yet).

To copy a table, follow these steps:

1. In the Navigation pane, select the table to copy.

2. Press Ctrl+C to copy it to the Clipboard.

3. Press Ctrl+V to paste it from the Clipboard. The Paste Table As dialog box opens.

4. Type a name for the table in the Table Name box, replacing the default name.

5. Choose whether to copy the Structure Only or the Structure and Data. See Figure 1-13.

6. Click OK.

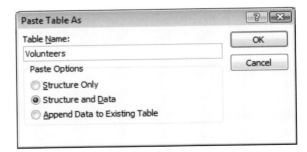

Figure 1-13
Copy a table.

This technique works to copy other objects as well, not just tables. You can use it to copy queries, forms, reports, and so on.

Entering and Viewing Data in a Datasheet

ONCE YOUR TABLE STRUCTURE has been defined, you are ready to enter data into the table. You can do this using forms you create (see Chapter 4), or you can type directly into a datasheet, just like you do with a spreadsheet in Excel. You can then navigate between records using Access's navigational controls or by sorting or searching for records.

Typing a Record into a Datasheet

To type a record into a datasheet:

1. Click in the first empty row, in the first (leftmost) column, and type an entry for that field.

> If the field contains (New), it is an AutoNumber field, which Access fills in for you. Press Tab to move to the next field.

2. Press Tab to move to the next field and type an entry for it, or press Tab to skip that field.

> You can skip any field except those that are set to be required. You will learn how to set a field to be required in Chapter 2.

3. Continue moving through the fields for that record until all have been filled in. When you get to the last field, pressing Tab moves you to the first field in a new row (record). See Figure 1-14.

Figure 1-14
Type records into a datasheet.

Unlike in other Office applications where you have to choose a Save command to save your work, Access automatically saves each record when you move to another record. You do not need to save unless you are making changes to the structure of the database, such as modifying field properties or creating new objects. However, you can save a record *without* moving away from it by choosing Home > Records > Save.

> Depending on the field type you choose (see Chapter 2), some fields may not be plain text boxes in which you enter data. There might be check boxes (for yes/no fields), for example, or a field with a drop-down list from which you select a preset value.

New records appear at the bottom of the datasheet. You cannot insert a new blank row in the midst of the existing records. However, you can sort the records in the datasheet by any field you like, as you will learn later in this chapter.

> **To quickly jump to the bottom of the datasheet and start a new record, you can choose Home > Records > New.**

Moving Through a Datasheet

To move through the datasheet, you can use the scroll bars, the same as with a spreadsheet in Excel. You can also use the navigation buttons at the bottom of the datasheet window. (These same navigation buttons appear at the bottom of a form, too, and are actually more useful for a form, since the form shows only one record at a time, so there is more need to switch from one record to another.)

The navigation buttons show the current record and the total number of records. You can type a record number in the specific record box and press Enter to move to that record. See Figure 1-15.

You can also use the arrow keys to move around the datasheet, and you can use a number of shortcut keys to move to specific points in the datasheet:

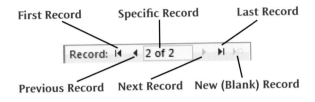

Figure 1-15
Datasheet navigation buttons

To Move To	Press
Next field to the right	Tab or Enter
Previous field to the left	Shift+Tab
Last field in the current row	End
First field in the current row	Home
Last field in last row	Ctrl+End
First field in first row	Ctrl+Home

Sorting Records in a Datasheet

Sorting reorders the records by one or more fields. Most types of fields can be sorted. You can sort in ascending order (A to Z or 1 to 9) or descending order (Z to A or 9 to 1). Some reasons to sort might include the following:

▶ **To see groups of data (for example, all clients who live in Illinois or all of yesterday's sales)**

▶ **To see information organized from smallest or largest values**

▶ **To group all records that have blanks in a certain field**

▶ **To scan for duplicate records**

Before sorting a datasheet, you must first move the insertion point into the field you want to sort (any record). For example, if you want to sort clients by last name, move to the Last Name field. Then choose Home > Sort & Filter > Ascending or Home > Sort & Filter > Descending. See Figure 1-16.

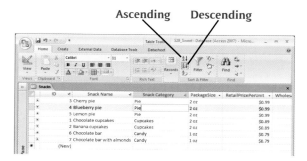

Figure 1-16
This data is sorted in descending order by Snack Category.

To return the records to their original order, re-sort by the ID field (or whatever field is the AutoNumbered field for the table), if there is one. If the table does not have a field that reflects the original entry order, an alternative is to close the table and, when prompted, choose No to not save the changes to it. You can also use the Undo button or Ctrl+Z to undo a sort, as long as you have not saved changes to the table.

Selecting Records

To select a single record, click the record selector button (the blank button immediately to the left of the record's leftmost field).

To select multiple contiguous records, select the first one and then hold down Shift as you click the record selector of the last one. You cannot select multiple non-contiguous records in a datasheet.

Record Selector

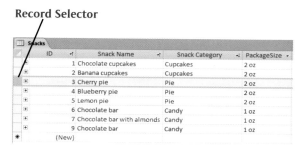

Figure 1-17
Select a record.

Copying and Moving Data in a Datasheet

To move and copy the contents of individual cells, use the Clipboard, just as in other Office programs. You can use any combination of the Cut, Copy, and Paste buttons or shortcut keys (Ctrl+X, Ctrl+C, and Ctrl+V, respectively).

You can also copy and paste entire records, providing they do not have any content that would create a situation where pasting would create a rule violation (such as having duplicate entries in a field that is set to be unique for each record). To copy and paste an entire record:

1. Click the record selector to select the entire record.

2. Press Ctrl+C to copy it to the Clipboard.

3. Click the row selector for the first empty row at the bottom of the datasheet (the one with the asterisk [*] symbol in the record selector area).

4. Press Ctrl+V to paste the record.

Editing Records

You may need to correct field information after you enter it. You can delete and add text in the same way you would in Word or Excel:

> ▶ **Click to position the insertion point. Press Backspace to remove text before the insertion point, or press Delete to remove text after the insertion point.**

> ▶ **Drag the mouse pointer to select text, and then press Delete to remove the selection or type to replace the selection with new text.**

> ▶ **Move the mouse point to the beginning (left) of a field so that the pointer changes to a white plus sign. Then click to select the entire contents of that cell.**

As you are making changes to a record, a pencil icon appears in the row selector area. The pencil indicates that any changes are not currently saved. They are saved when you leave that record, either by closing the datasheet or moving the insertion point into a different record. If you want to undo your changes before they are saved, you can press Esc. If you want to undo your changes after they are saved, press Ctrl+Z or click the Undo button on the Quick Access toolbar.

Deleting Records

Access shows the total number of records in the datasheet in the navigation buttons at the bottom of the window.

You can delete the current record or one or more contiguous records. Once you delete a record, it is gone forever; you cannot use Undo to reverse the action, and the change is saved immediately.

To delete a record (or multiple records), select the record(s), and then do any of the following:

> ▶ **Press the Delete key on the keyboard.**

> ▶ **Right-click the selection and click Delete Record.**

> ▶ **Choose Datasheet > Records > Delete.**

Access displays a warning message. Click OK to confirm the deletion.

If you have an AutoNumber field in the table, when you delete a record, Access will not reuse the numbers of the deleted records. That is why an AutoNumber field might not appear consecutively numbered in all cases.

Creating and
Editing Tables

USING JUST THE SKILLS YOU GAINED from Chapter 1, you can use Access to store data. If your database needs are simple, and you are not too picky about the fields being the right types, sizes, and formats, you can get by. But wouldn't it be nice if the fields were a little more orderly? For example, suppose you have a field that stores the prices of items; wouldn't it be nice to see those prices in a currency format, with two decimal places?

In this chapter, you will learn how to use **Table Design view**, a very powerful view that enables you to edit, format, and assign properties to the fields in a table. You'll learn how to set field types, change the lengths of text-based fields, make certain fields required or indexed, add captions, and more.

Editing a Table Design in Design View

THERE ARE MANY WAYS OF opening a table in Design view. If the table is already open in Datasheet view, you can do any of the following:

- ▶ **Right-click the datasheet's tab and choose Design View.**

- ▶ **In the Navigation pane, right-click the table name and choose Design View.**

- ▶ **Choose Datasheet > Views > View. There are two ways to go here. A Design View button appears by default here when Datasheet view is open, and you can simply click that button. Alternatively, you can click the down arrow below the button and click Design View from the menu that appears. See Figure 2-1.**

That last method also works if the table is not open.

In Design view, a table appears in two panes. In the upper pane is a field list, with each field in its own row. In the lower pane is a tabbed properties sheet where the properties of the currently selected field appear. See Figure 2-2.

Changing the Field Type

The Data Type column in the upper pane in Design view tells you what type of information the field can store. Click the drop-down arrow in this cell to choose from the list of data types. You can also type the first letter of the data type to make this choice, if you prefer to use the keyboard. Table 2-1 lists and describes the data types.

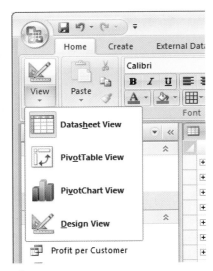

Figure 2-1
Entering Design view

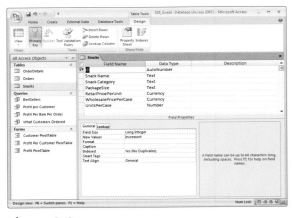

Figure 2-2
Table Design view

Table 2-1 Field Data Types in Access 2007

Data Type	Description
Text	Includes any characters up to a maximum of 255 (determined by field size). If the data includes a mix of numbers and any amount of letters, choose this field type. Examples include name and address fields. Phone numbers, Social Security numbers, and ZIP codes are also usually assigned this type, even though they contain only digits, because the entries in these fields will never need to be used in math formulas.
Memo	Use this type when Text is not large enough. Like Text, this type can also have letters and numbers but can be much larger, up to 65,536 characters. Don't use Memo unless you need that extra length, however, because you can't perform certain actions (indexing, for example) on a Memo field.
Number	Includes various forms of numerical data that can be used in calculations.
Date/Time	Date and time entries in formats showing the date only, the time only, or both.
Currency	Use for currency values with up to four digits after the decimal point. This data type is more accurate for large numbers than the Number data type, but it generally takes up more space.
AutoNumber	Usually this is used to create an ID number for each record. The value for each record increments by one.
Yes/No	Only two possible values can be in this field. You can set the field options to appear as Yes/No, True/False, or On/Off. The default style shows a check box rather than a text value.
OLE Object	This data type enables you to place another file into your record. Within the field, you can insert a picture (a logo, for example), a Word document, an Excel spreadsheet, and so on. On forms and reports, you can create controls that allow the object to appear. For example, if you use such a field to store photos of employees, you could create a report that showed each employee's picture next to his or her name.
Hyperlink	This type allows you to insert a Web address that will launch a browser window when you click it in Datasheet view or on a form or report. You could also type a path and file name to a file on your hard disk or a network drive in a hyperlink field. The important point here is that the text opens up another location or document when clicked.
Attachment	This new data type, available only in Access 2007 databases, allows the storage of external content, much like an OLE field does. However, it does not display the content in Access; it shows a paperclip icon for the content. Another difference is that this field type allows you to store multiple attachments per record, and you can store any type of file, not just one for which the PC has an associated application. (There are a few exceptions; you can't store "dangerous" file types, like .js, .bat., and .asp, because those types of files can carry viruses and other malware.)
Lookup Wizard	This is not actually a field type but a link to a wizard that enables you to create a lookup from which you can choose when entering data. After choosing this type and running the wizard, you end up with a field type of Text or Number, depending on the data. Chapter 3 covers lookups.

> Each type of object has its own Design view. So there is Table Design view, Report Design view, and so on. Often in this book, as a shortcut, I will refer to the view simply as Design view when it is obvious what type of object we are working with.

Using Field Descriptions

Field descriptions are optional. You can enter anything you want here, but most people use it to provide comments or hints about the intended use and/or limitations of the field. This information will be seen primarily by any other Access database designers who work with your file.

Changing a Field Name

To change a field's name, edit the entry in the Field Name column. Although you may use up to 64 characters for a field name, you should try to keep the names short so they are easier to work with and so they are not truncated when they appear as column headings in a datasheet.

Adding and Deleting Fields

To add another field, type it in the first empty row of the grid in the upper section of Design view. This places the new field at the bottom of the field list (to the far right end of the datasheet in Datasheet view).

If you would like the new field in some other position than the last, follow these steps:

1. Select the row for the field above which the new one should appear. To select a row, click the row selector, which is the blank square to the right of the field name.

2. Choose Design > Tools > Insert Rows. A new blank row appears, in which you can type the new field. See Figure 2-3.

To delete a field, select its row (again, with the row selector) and choose Design > Tools > Delete Rows.

Row selector

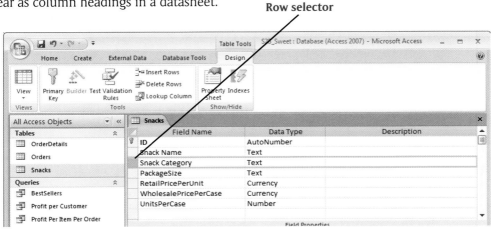

Figure 2-3
Insert a field.

You can have field names that include spaces, but sometimes such field names will cause problems when working with advanced operations and when exporting data to other programs. Therefore, it is generally a good idea to make field names all one word, running multiple words together and using capitalization to separate them, such as FirstName. You can then use a field caption to make an alternative wording appear in the column headings. See "Specifying a Caption" later in this chapter.

Reordering Fields

Fields appear in Datasheet view in the order listed in Design view. Top to bottom in Design view equals left to right in the datasheet.

To reorder the fields, follow these steps:

1. Select a field by clicking its row selector in the upper portion of Table Design view.

2. Drag the field up or down on the list. A thick horizontal line shows where it is going, as shown in Figure 2-4. Release the mouse button when the line is where you want the field to be moved.

Field being moved   **Mouse pointer**   **Line shows destination**

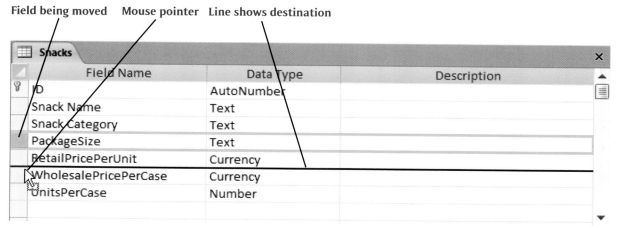

Figure 2-4
Rearrange fields by dragging them.

Specifying the Primary Key Field

EACH TABLE SHOULD HAVE a field in which each record will be unique, such as an ID number field. This field will be the table's **primary key**. In some tables this is an AutoNumber field, where Access assigns the unique ID number automatically (starting with 1 for the first record), but this is not required; the primary key field can even be a text field (such as a part number that includes letters and numbers).

To specify the primary key for the table, follow these steps:

1. Select the field in the top pane of Design view.

2. Choose Design > Tools > Primary Key. A key symbol appears in the row selector area to indicate that it is the primary key. See Figure 2-5.

To choose a different field as the primary key, repeat that for some other field. To turn primary key usage off entirely, select the field that is already the primary key and choose Design > Tools > Primary Key again.

In some cases, there might not be a single field that must be unique for every record. Instead, each record might need to have a unique combination of values in two or more fields. For example, in a table called Student Registration, each record might require a unique combination of Student ID and Class ID. To set up the primary key in such a table, select both of the fields at once (hold down Ctrl as you click the second one) before clicking the Primary Key button.

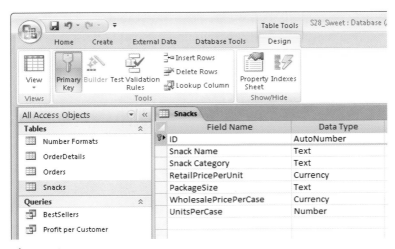

Figure 2-5
Choose a primary key field for the table.

Defining Field Properties

WHEN A FIELD IS SELECTED in the upper pane of Design view (that is, when the insertion point is in any part of its row), properties for that field appear in the lower pane. There are two tabs: General and Lookup. General is the home of almost all of the settings you will use; Lookup is a special-purpose tab that you'll learn more about in Chapter 3.

The properties available depend on the field type; not all field types have all the properties covered in this chapter.

The following sections show some of the most commonly used properties for Text, Number, and other common data types.

Setting a Field Size

By default, all Text fields are 255 characters in length. In other words, you can type up to 255 characters per record in those fields. You cannot increase this size, but you can decrease it.

If you need a text field that is larger than 255 characters, use the Memo type.

You might want to decrease the field's size for one of these reasons:

▶ **To control the values that are entered into the field to create some standardization of input. For example, you might limit the State field to two characters to prevent users from entering the full state names.**

▶ **To decrease the size of the database file. Each field and record occupies a certain amount of disk space, even if all the space isn't used. For example, if you leave the FirstName field set to 255 characters, and you have 100 records, that's 100 times 255 times 1 byte of disk space, or 25,500 bytes just for that one field. Decreasing that field size to 20 characters would decrease the database file size by 23,500 bytes. Do that for all your fields, eliminating the extraneous space, and you can dramatically decrease the size of the database, and the savings keep coming with each new record.**

After decreasing a field's size, you won't see a change in the database file size until you run a Compact and Repair operation on the database file. To do that, choose Office > Manage > Compact & Repair Database.

To change the field size, enter a different number in the Field Size property on the General tab. See Figure 2-6.

For a field with the Number data type, you can also set the field size, but rather than a specific value, you choose from among the sizes in Table 2-2.

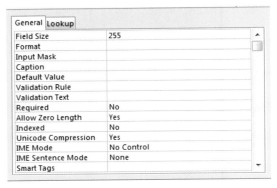

Figure 2-6
Change the field size.

Table 2-2 Field Sizes for the Number Data Type

Field Size	Range of Values Stored	Comments
Byte	Integers from 0 to 255	Takes up the least space; only 1 byte needed to store field value.
Integer	Integers from −32,768 to 32,767	Occupies 2 bytes of space per record.
Long Integer	Integers from −2,147,483,648 to 2,147,483,647	Occupies 4 bytes of space per record. Use this type when creating a field that will have a relationship to another table's AutoNumber primary key field to avoid possible problems with running out of numbers in a very large database.
Single	Numeric floating point values (all numbers, not just integers) that range from -3.4×10^{38} to 3.4×10^{38} and up to seven significant digits	Occupies 4 bytes of space per record.
Double	Numeric floating point values that range from -1.797×10^{308} to 1.797×10^{308} and up to 15 significant digits	Occupies 8 bytes of space per record.
Replication ID	For storing a GUID (an ID that is required for replication)	Special-purpose; infrequently used. Occupies 16 bytes per record.
Decimal	For numeric values that range from -9.999×10^{27} to 9.999×10^{27}	Occupies 12 bytes per record.

Selecting a Field Format

The field Format property helps you present field values (primarily numeric ones) in a certain way. For numeric fields, the field Format property is a drop-down list from which you can choose, as shown in Figure 2-7. Table 2-3 shows examples of the various formats.

The number of decimal places is a separate setting from the number type, and is set in the Decimal Places property.

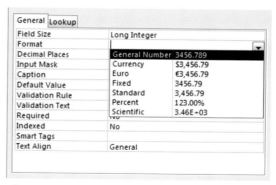

Figure 2-7
Select a field format for a numeric field.

Table 2-3 Formats for Numeric Fields

Format	Example given input of 0123456.7890	Comments
General Number	123456.789	Displays up to 11 digits to the right of left of the decimal point. Access rounds the number if you set a specific number of decimal places in the Decimal Places property, or shows all decimal places of that property if set to Auto. If there are more than 10 digits to the right or left of the decimal point, this format appears the same as Scientific Notation.
Currency	$123,456.79	Applies the currency symbol and format specified in your Windows regional settings.
Euro	€ 123,456.79	Uses the Euro symbol, rather than the default currency symbol, but otherwise uses the currency formatting specified in your Windows regional settings.
Fixed	123456.79	Displays numbers without thousands separators, and with two decimal places. Access displays a rounded version of the number if more than two decimal places are input, but stores the exact value entered behind the scenes.
Standard	123,456.79	Displays numbers with thousands separators and two decimal places. Rounding behavior is same as with Fixed.
Percent	123456.79%	Displays numbers as percentages with two decimal places and a trailing percent sign. Rounding behavior is the same as with Fixed.
Scientific	1.23E+05	Displays numbers in scientific (exponential) notation. This consists of the number with the decimal point moved such that there is one digit before it and all the others trailing it, and then an E+ and the number of places the decimal point was moved.

Some of the numeric field sizes do not support decimal places, such as Integer; if you choose one of those field sizes, regardless of the number of decimal places you specify in the Decimal Places property, only integers will be stored.

For dates and times, the Format property controls whether the date, the time, or both will appear, and in what form. Table 2-4 lists the available formats for a Date/Time field. Each format uses the separator characters specified in your Regional settings in Windows.

To access the Regional settings in Windows Vista, choose Start > Control Panel > Clock, Language, and Region > Regional and Language Options, and click Customize This Format.

Table 2-4 Formats for Date/Time Fields

Format	Example	Comments
General Date	01/01/2009 09:10:30 AM	Displays dates as numbers and time values as hours, minutes, and seconds, followed by AM or PM. If the value has no time, it displays only the date; if it has no date, it displays only the time.
Long Date	Thursday, January 1, 2009	Displays only the date value, as specified by the Long Date format in your Windows Regional settings.
Medium Date	01-January-2009	Displays the date as dd/month/yyyy.
Short Date	01/01/2009	Displays the date as specified by the Short Date format in your Windows Regional settings.
Long Time	09:10:30 AM	Displays the hours, minutes, and seconds, followed by AM or PM.
Medium Time	09:10 AM	Displays the hours and minutes, followed by AM or PM.
Short Time	09:10	Displays only hours and minutes (no AM or PM).

Specifying a Caption

If you follow the guideline mentioned earlier in this chapter about avoiding spaces in field names, you may run into a dilemma in that some fields are more understandable if they have multi-word names, but the words look awkward if you run them together as in FirstName.

You can get around this problem by assigning field names that follow the rules but then assigning captions to the fields that are more readable. A *caption* appears as the column heading in Datasheet view and as a label for the field when it appears on a form or report. Enter a caption in the Caption property for the field. All field types have this property available. See Figure 2-8.

General	Lookup	
Format	Currency	
Decimal Places	Auto	
Input Mask		
Caption	Price Per Unit	
Default Value		
Validation Rule		
Validation Text		
Required	No	
Indexed	No	
Smart Tags		
Text Align	General	

Figure 2-8
Enter a caption to appear as a label for the field on datasheets, forms, and reports.

Specifying a Default Value

If almost all your records have the same value for a particular field, you can save some data entry time by assigning a default value to that field. The default value appears automatically in that field for each new record and can be changed whenever needed. Set it in the Default Value property.

Making a Field Required

When a field is required, you have to enter something in it in order to save the record. AutoNumber fields are always required (Access does the entry for you, so you can't help it), as are primary key fields. Everything else is set to Non-Required by default. You can require a field by changing the Required field value to Yes.

Forcing a Field to Contain Unique Values

If each record must have a different value for a particular field, you can set the Indexed property to Yes (No Duplicates) to have Access disallow any duplicate entries. AutoNumber and primary key fields are always unique-valued.

3

Improving Table Design and Creating
Relationships

PICTURE YOUR CAREFULLY DESIGNED database put into a production environment, where other people are using it to enter and edit data. They might not have the same computer expertise as you, and might not be as careful and consistent as you might want them to be, so they might make typos, enter the same value in different ways (such as entering IN, IND, or Indiana to represent the same state). There are some ways to make it harder for users to mess up your data, though, and in this chapter you will learn about three of them: input masks, data validation, and lookups. In this chapter, you will also learn how to create relationships between tables so you can start building more complex database systems.

Setting Up Input Masks

AN INPUT MASK IS LIKE A FRAME that the data is poured into. It makes sure that you enter the correct number and type of characters. For example, the Phone Number input mask ensures that you enter exactly 10 digits. Input masks also provide helper symbols that make the data display in a more understandable way. For phone numbers, it adds parentheses around the first three digits (the area code) and adds a dash between the remaining three and four digits, like this: (317) 555-5555.

Input masks work only with fields with the Text, Date/Time, Number, and Currency data types. To restrict entries in other field types, you must use validation rules, covered later in this chapter.

When you add an input mask to a table field, any future forms you create based on that table will use that input mask. However, any existing forms based on that table are not affected (unless you delete the affected field from the form and reinsert it).

Using the Input Mask Wizard

The easiest way to create an input mask is to use the Input Mask Wizard (see Figure 3-1). It walks you step by step through the process of creating the codes necessary for the mask in the Input Mask property for the field.

The Input Mask Wizard works only with Text and Date/Time fields; if you want an input mask for a Number or Currency field, you must create it manually, described in the next section.

Follow these steps to create an input mask with the wizard:

1. Select the field in the upper pane of Table Design view.

2. In the lower pane, click in the Input Mask field.

3. Click the Build button (looks like three dots) to the right of the Input Mask field. The Wizard runs.

4. Select the type of mask you want to create. You can choose from several common mask types, including Phone Number, Social Security Number, and ZIP Code.

5. Click Finish to accept the default for that input mask type.

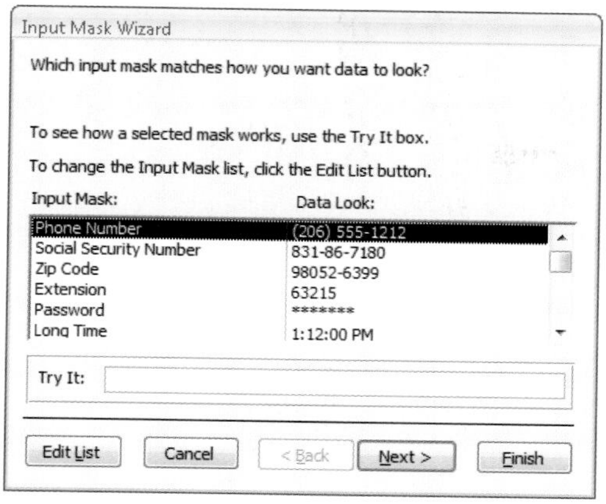

Again, you have the option of clicking Finish to end the wizard or clicking Next to continue. If you continue, you will be asked how you want the data stored in the database: with or without the helper characters. If you are just going to use the data in Access, it makes no difference, because the input mask will show the helper characters whether or not they are an actual part of the stored data. If you export the data to another format, however, such as a text file, it makes a difference. See Figure 3-3. Then click Finish to end the wizard.

Figure 3-1
Choose an input mask type.

Instead of clicking Finish in step 5, you can click Next instead, and then fine-tune the input mask by changing the codes and/or choosing a different placeholder character. See Figure 3-2. The codes will make more sense to you after you read the following section.

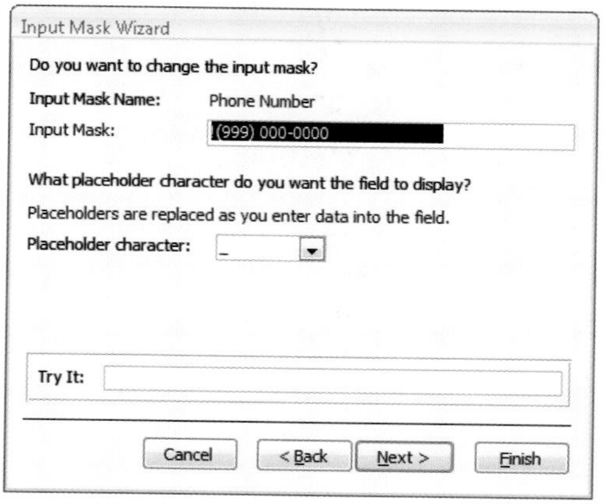

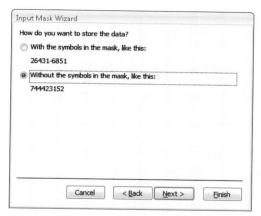

Figure 3-3
Choose how the data is stored in the database.

After you've completed the wizard, the code for the input mask appears in the Input Mask field. The next section explains how to interpret these codes and how to edit them.

Figure 3-2
Customize the input mask, if desired.

Creating a Custom Input Mask

You can enter your own input mask by typing characters in a specified format directly into the Input Mask text box; you can also edit any existing codes that were placed there by the wizard. Entering codes directly is the only way of creating an input mask for a Number or Currency field.

There are up to three sections for the input mask. Sections are separated with semicolons.

▶ **The first section consists of the input mask characters.**

▶ **The second section stores extra characters, such as parentheses.**

▶ **The third section indicates the character to use as filler before the data is entered.**

Table 3-1 shows the characters to use for the first section of the input mask; Table 3-2 shows the characters for the second section.

For example, an input mask for a 5-digit ZIP code might look something like this: 00000;;_. The 00000 specifies five required digits. The semicolon marks the end of the first section. The second section is empty, so another semicolon immediately follows. The underscore (_) character indicates blanks to be filled.

The input mask !"("999") "999"-"9999 allows you to put numbers anywhere in the field. If you only enter seven numbers, even at the beginning of the field, the numbers will display to the right of the parentheses. For example, as you enter the number, it will show (555) 456-7 but after the number is entered, it will display as ( ) 555-4567.

Table 3-1 Characters for the First Section of the Input Mask

Data	Description	Entry Required	Entry Optional
Number	0 to 9, no + or – signs	0	9
Number or space	Leading and trailing spaces are blanks but removed when field is saved. + and – are allowed.		#
Letter	A to Z	L	?
Letter or number	A to Z or 0 to 9	A	a
Any character or space		&	C

Table 3-2 Characters for the Second Section of the Input Mask

Period (.), comma (,), colon (:), semicolon (;), hyphen (-), and slash (/)	Decimal, thousand, date, and time separators, depending on Windows regional settings.
!	Causes characters to fill on the right side of the field after you leave the field.
\	Any character following is displayed.
" "	Any characters within quotes are displayed.
>	Converts following characters to uppercase.
<	Converts following characters to lowercase.

If you click in a field with an input mask in Datasheet view, you will be entering data at a specific position in the input mask, which is not necessarily the beginning. This may cause errors if you have required characters. You can press Home to get to the beginning of the field. Or, to avoid errors such as these, instead of clicking in the field to move the insertion point into it, press Tab from the field immediately before it to enter the field.

An input mask does not affect data already in the table. If you change an input mask property after data is entered and want to use the input mask to validate each character, delete the entire contents of the field for that record and retype its entry.

Using Data Validation

INPUT MASKS CAN FORCE the user to enter a certain number or type of characters, but it cannot restrict the content of the field. That's where a data validation rule comes in. With a **data validation rule**, you can create criteria that must be met for a field value to be accepted. A validation rule looks not just at the characters in the entry, but also the value of the entry. For example, it can ensure that a date entered is within a certain range.

> Unlike an input mask, which tests each character as you enter it, a validation rule evaluates the data as you exit the field.

To create a data validation rule, you type a code representing the rule in the Data Validation property for the field. Then you enter a custom error message in the Validation Text box that will appear when the rule has been violated. Figure 3-4 shows an example.

> Null is not the same as zero; zero is a value. Null is a lack of value.

General	Lookup
Format	Currency
Decimal Places	Auto
Input Mask	
Caption	Price Per Unit
Default Value	
Validation Rule	<100
Validation Text	All units must cost less than $100
Required	No
Indexed	No
Smart Tags	
Text Align	General

Figure 3-4
Enter data validation properties.

Most validation rules use relational operators. These are math operators that compare one expression to another. Here are some basic ones:

>	Greater than
<	Less than
>=	Greater than or equal to
<=	Less than or equal to
<>	Not equal to
=	Equal to

For text strings, Access also uses the word "like" as a relational operator. For example, Like "???" would restrict a text entry to exactly three characters. Validation rules can have compound conditions with the use of AND and OR.

Access uses the word "Null" to mean empty. You can use it in validation rules to refer to the quality of a cell being without any entry in it.

Here are some examples of validation rules:

>1/1/09	After January 1, 2009
Between 1/1/09 and 12/31/09	Any date in 2009
<=100	Less than or equal to 100
Is Null or In "("CO","OR","CA","NM")	Is blank or one of the states CO, OR, CA, or NM
"Denver" or "Boise"	Denver or Boise (can't be blank)
<>0	Any non-zero value
Like "E????"	Any five-character entry that begins with E

When digits are entered in a Text field, they are considered alphabetic characters and can be placed in alphabetical order. Numbers 0 through 9 come before the letter A alphabetically. Therefore, a validation rule such as this:

```
Like "???" and >="LA1" and <="LA3"
```

would allow only values of LA1, LA2, or LA3 to be entered. However, if the validation rule was

```
>="LA1" and <="LA3"
```

then the entry could be any number of characters as long as the entry began with LA1, LA2, or LA3.

If the data does not match the validation rule, a generic error message appears unless you have created a custom error message. You can enter custom error messages in the Validation Text property.

If you change the validation rule after you've entered text in a table, Access will offer to check the existing data to make sure it follows the rule (see Figure 3-5).

When entering new records, an error will appear (either the generic or custom one), and you will not be allowed to save the record until you change the offending condition.

Figure 3-5
Existing data can be validated with the new rule.

A lookup field would be perfect for a situation like the one in the preceding examples, where the entries are restricted to a few specific values. Lookups are covered later in this chapter.

Multiple Field Validation

Validation rules entered for individual fields apply only to those fields. If you want to create a validation rule that relies on more than one field, such as comparing the values of one field to another, you must enter the validation rule in the properties for the table itself.

To set up a multi-field validation rule, follow these steps:

1. Choose Design > Show/Hide > Property Sheet.

2. Create the validation rule in the Validation Rule property in the Property Sheet task pane that appears. See Figure 3-6.

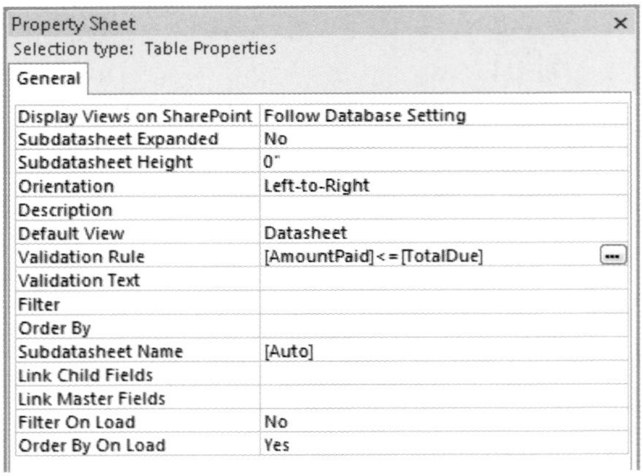

To refer to field names in a multi-field rule, enclose them in square brackets. In Figure 3-6, for example, the rule specifies that the AmountPaid value must be less than or equal to the TotalDue value.

For a multi-field validation, the rule is not checked, and the error does not appear until the user leaves the record rather than the individual field.

Property Sheet		×
Selection type: Table Properties		
General		
Display Views on SharePoint	Follow Database Setting	
Subdatasheet Expanded	No	
Subdatasheet Height	0"	
Orientation	Left-to-Right	
Description		
Default View	Datasheet	
Validation Rule	[AmountPaid]<=[TotalDue]	...
Validation Text		
Filter		
Order By		
Subdatasheet Name	[Auto]	
Link Child Fields		
Link Master Fields		
Filter On Load	No	
Order By On Load	Yes	

Figure 3-6
Create a multi-field validation rule.

Creating a Lookup

I F YOU HAVE SEVERAL VALUES that can appear in a field, consider using a lookup field. It can help prevent user entry errors by enabling users to select from a list of values rather than making them retype the entry each time, and it also pleases users by helping them save time. Figure 3-7 shows an example of a lookup field.

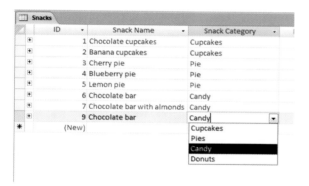

Figure 3-7
A lookup simplifies data entry.

It is possible to set up a lookup manually on the Lookup tab for the field's properties, but it is much easier to use the Lookup Wizard to do so.

A lookup can either present values that you manually enter or present values drawn from another table. Neither is necessarily better; it just depends on the situation. If there are many values to choose from, and they are already entered in an existing table, it is easier to reference them from that other table than to retype them.

Referencing another table is also advantageous if the values in the list should change as records are added or deleted from that table. On the other hand, if you have only a few values that the user should choose from, and they do not exist anywhere else in the database, entering them in the Lookup Wizard is the best way.

Create a Value List with the Lookup Wizard

The Lookup Wizard provides a list in which you can type the values you want to appear on the drop-down list on the datasheet or form. This method works well when the values on the list will seldom or never change (such as choosing between Male and Female for sex). If the values change frequently, use the table lookup method instead, covered in the next section.

Follow these steps to create a lookup that contains a list you create yourself:

1. In Design view, open the Data Type drop-down list for a field and choose Lookup Wizard.

2. Choose I Will Type In the Values That I Want, and click Next.

3. Type the items to appear on the list, one item per row. Use only a single column. See Figure 3-8. Then click Next.

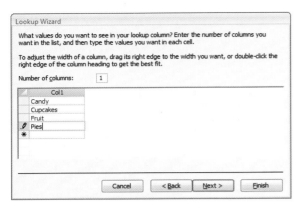

Figure 3-8
Create a lookup by typing the list values.

4. If desired, change the name of the field. See Figure 3-9. Any change you make here is applied to the entry in the Field Name column for the field—it changes its actual name, not just its caption.

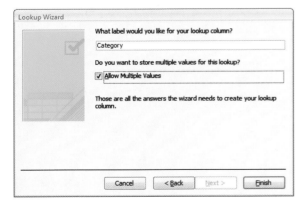

Figure 3-9
Choose a different name for the field if desired, and whether or not to allow multiple values.

5. If desired, mark the Allow Multiple Values check box. (See the following note for guidance on that decision.)

6. Click Finish.

7. If you marked the check box in step 5, a warning appears that you will not be able to go back to using single values for this field after you save the table. Click Yes.

> **Allowing multiple values per field is a new feature in Access 2007. If you enable this option, users will be able to select from a check box–style list, and mark more than one value for each record. This can be handy in certain situations, such as when describing multiple skills that an employee has. However, don't use that option unless it's pertinent to the field you are working with because it renders the database incompatible with previous versions of Access.**

8. Choose Design > Views > View to switch to Datasheet view.

9. When prompted to save the table, click Yes.

10. Check the lookup in Datasheet view to make sure it is working correctly. If it isn't, go back to Design view (Datasheet > Views > View) and recreate the lookup.

Create a Value List from a Table

If the list often varies, you are better off creating a separate table for the list instead, and then creating a lookup that looks into that table.

Before setting up the lookup, then, you must first create the additional table. It needs only one field in it—the field that will contain the entries. After creating the table, enter records for each list item. Finally, after that setup, run the Lookup Wizard.

> Creating a lookup with a table creates a relationship between the tables, which will be reflected in the Relationships window. You will learn about relationships later in this chapter.

To use a table for a lookup, follow these steps:

1. In Design view, open the Data Type drop-down list for a field and choose Lookup Wizard.

2. Click I Want the Lookup Column to Look Up the Values in a Table or Query, and click Next.

3. Click the table (or query) that has the field containing the list. See Figure 3-10. Then click Next.

4. Select the field to use, and click the > button to move it to the Selected Fields list. See Figure 3-11. (In Figure 3-11, there is only one field, and it has not yet been moved over.) Then click Next.

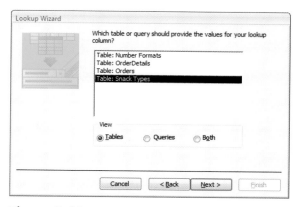

Figure 3-10
Select the source table/query for the list.

> If the table you choose for the lookup has a primary key field, and the field you are using for the list isn't it, it's a good idea to choose it, too. Then you can hide the primary key field in the lookup. The users will choose from the "friendly" field, such as the text names, but the actual entry in the table will be the unique primary key value for that choice.

Figure 3-11
Select the field that contains the values for the lookup.

5. (Optional) If you want the list sorted, open the 1 drop-down list and select the field name (see Figure 3-12). The default sort order is Ascending; if you prefer Descending, click the Ascending button to toggle it. Then click Next.

Figure 3-12
Select a sort field.

6. If desired, drag the right border of the sample column that appears to adjust the width of the lookup list. You might need to widen it if any of the entries are too long to fit in the default column width. Then click Next.

7. If desired, change the name of the field. (Refer back to Figure 3-9; this is the same as in the previous section.)

8. If desired, mark the Allow Multiple Values check box. (See the note in the previous section about multiple values.)

9. Click Finish.

10. If you marked the check box in step 8, a warning appears that you will not be able to go back to using single values for this field after you save the table. Click Yes.

11. When prompted to save the table before relationships can be created, click Yes.

12. Choose Design > Views > View to switch to Datasheet view.

13. When prompted to save the table, click Yes.

14. Check the lookup in Datasheet view to make sure it is working correctly. If it isn't, go back to Design view (Datasheet > Views > View) and recreate the lookup.

> If you have existing text values in a field that you are converting to a lookup field, and the new lookup will contain the numeric ID numbers from the corresponding table rather than the values, creating the lookup will delete all the non-numeric previous entries in that field, and you will need to reenter them. For this reason, it's best to set up any lookups before you do much data entry.

Creating Relationships

WHEN YOU HAVE MULTIPLE tables in a database, there is probably some sort of relationship between them logically. For example, in a database for a veterinary office, you might have a table for Customers and a table for Pets, with each record in the Pets table representing an animal owned by someone in the Customers table. You might further have a table called Services Offered and another one called Services Performed. Services Performed might reference the pet that was seen and the service that was performed. Figure 3-13 shows the Relationships window for such a database, with lines between the tables indicating the relationships.

Figure 3-13
A sample database with relationships between the tables

Notice how each relationship in Figure 3-13 runs from the primary key in one table to a non-primary-key field (the **foreign key**) in another table. This is not required, but it is customary. The entry in the related field is unique on one side but not on the other, such as Customers and Pets. A customer can have more than one pet, but a pet can have only one owner. The same thing with Pets and Services Performed.

Each pet has a unique ID number, but can receive multiple services. This is called a **one-to-many relationship**. Notice also the symbols on the relationship lines in Figure 3-13. Next to the "one" side is a 1; next to the "many" side is an infinity symbol (a sideways 8). The table that contains the primary key is called the **parent table**, and the table that contains the foreign key is called the **child table**.

> In most cases, the related fields must have the same field type (Text, Number, and so on). The one exception is, if the primary key field is an AutoNumber type, the related field on the "many" side must be a Number type.

Displaying the Relationships Window and Adding Tables

You set up relationships in the Relationships window. Follow these steps to open it and add tables to it:

1. Choose Database Tools > Show/Hide > Relationships.

2. If the Show Table dialog box does not automatically appear, choose Design > Relationships > Show Table.

3. Double-click a table to add it to the Relationships window. Repeat as needed to add more tables. See Figure 3-14.

4. Click Close.

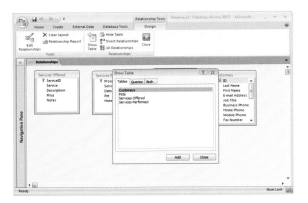

Figure 3-14
Adding tables to the Relationships window

Each table appears as a list of fields in a floating window. You can rearrange the tables in the Relationships window by dragging the title bar of the floating window. It makes no difference how they are arranged, except that it might make them easier for you to work with.

When you exit from the Relationship window, you are prompted to save your changes. If you want to revert back to the relationships you had when you opened the window, you can choose not to save them.

> **Think carefully about the relationship you want to create. The related fields must contain the same data; otherwise, there is no point in the relationship.**

Creating a Relationship

Some relationships are created automatically for you. For example, when you set up a lookup using values from another table, Access creates a relationship between those two tables, and if you add them both to the Relationships window, you will see a line connecting them.

Other relationships you must create yourself. To create a relationship:

1. Drag-and-drop between the field in one table and the corresponding field in the other table. The Edit Relationships dialog box opens. See Figure 3-15.

2. Accept the default settings, or make any changes to the settings needed. You will learn about the Enforce Referential Integrity setting in the next section.

3. Click Create. The dialog box closes and a connecting line appears between the two tables.

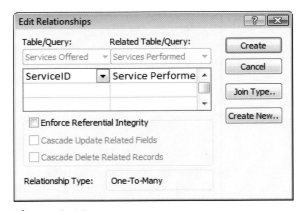

Figure 3-15
Create a relationship.

Enforcing Referential Integrity

Enforcing **referential integrity** can help users avoid errors by making it impossible for them to enter a value in one table that does not have a corresponding value in the related table. For example, if you enforced referential integrity between the Services Offered and Services Performed tables, users would not be able to record that a service had been performed unless that service was listed in the Services Offered table.

If you select Enforce Referential Integrity in the Edit Relationships dialog box (refer to Figure 3-15), you can choose two additional options: Cascade Update Related Fields and Cascade Delete Related Fields.

Cascade Update Related Fields means that when you change the value in the primary key of the parent table, the related foreign key field in all related records of the child table will automatically change as well. For example, if you changed the ServiceID value for a particular service in the Services Offered table, all the records that referenced that service would update in the Services Performed table. If you don't check this box, Access will give an error message when you try to change the primary key value.

Cascade Delete Related Records means that when you delete the record in the parent table, all related records in the child table will delete as well. For example, if you stopped offering a particular service and deleted it from the Services Offered table, all the records of pets that received that service would be deleted from the Services Performed table. (In that particular example, you would probably not want to use Cascade Delete because it would remove valuable information from the pets' medical records.)

If you don't mark this check box, Access will show an error message when you try to delete the record in the parent table.

Editing a Relationship

You can change a relationship between two tables after initially establishing it. Double-click the connector line between the two tables to reopen the Edit Relationships dialog box (refer to Figure 3-15). From there you can change the Referential Integrity settings.

Removing a Relationship

If you make a mistake when creating a relationship, you might need to remove it. To do so, select the connector line between the two tables so that the line becomes bold, and then press the Delete key on the keyboard. Click Yes to confirm.

Showing Related Records

You can view the parent table and the child table in Datasheet view. After you create a relationship between tables, display the parent table in Datasheet view and click on the plus sign on the left edge of a record to see the related rows from the child table. See Figure 3-16.

Figure 3-16
See records from the related table.

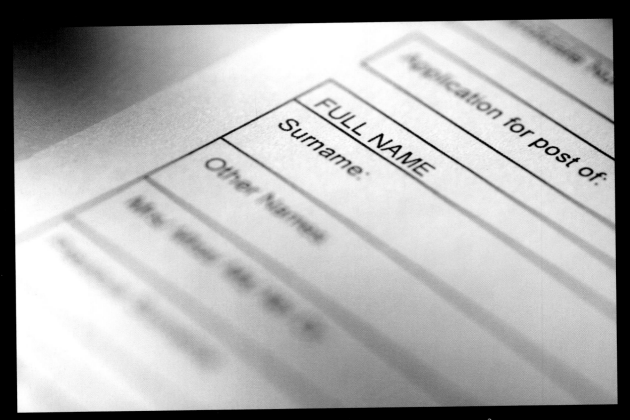

Creating
Forms

NOW THAT YOU HAVE CREATED a working database, picture it going "into production" where other people are using it for their daily work. Picture someone without much computer experience, facing a table containing thousands of data records, and feeling quite intimidated. You're not going to be there to reassure them or teach them how to use the table, so what can you do? Now picture the same user opening up the database and finding a friendly fill-in-the-blanks form to use for data entry. Insulated from the inner workings of the database, the user sees only what he or she needs to see.

Forms are not just for novices, though. Experienced users can benefit from using forms to enter and edit data because they make it easier for the eye to scan for the desired fields. In this chapter, you will learn several ways of creating and editing simple forms that you can use for data entry.

Creating a Data Entry Form

FORM IS A VIEW OF THE data from a table. Some forms can show data from multiple tables at once, with a subform embedded in the main form.

The most common type of form shows only one record at a time. It resembles a paper form you might fill out, with boxes in which to enter the values for each field. Figure 4-1 shows such a form. This is the kind of form you will be creating in this chapter. Other form types include those that resemble datasheets and those that display multiple records, one after the other, in a continuously scrolling version of Figure 4-1.

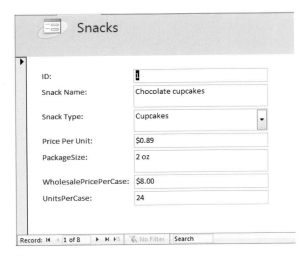

Figure 4-1
A typical form

Creating an Automatically Generated Form

The easiest way to create a form is to use the Form button on the Create tab. It creates a simple form based on whatever table or query was selected when you clicked it. In earlier versions of Access, such forms were called AutoForms; Access 2007 no longer uses that terminology, but the concept is the same.

Follow these steps to automatically generate a form:

1. In the Navigation pane, click the table or query on which to base the form.

2. Choose Create > Forms > Form.

If that table has a related table (for example, the Orders table is related to Order Details), Access automatically creates a subform with fields from the related table. Figure 4-2 shows such an example. Otherwise, it creates a simple form like the one in Figure 4-1. (The form in Figure 4-1 has been reformatted slightly from the default; you will learn how to format a form later in this chapter.)

There are several other buttons in the Create > Forms group for special-purpose forms. You may want to experiment with these on your own:

▶ **Split Form: Creates a form with two different viewing panes. One displays the form in single-record view, as in Figure 4-1; the other one displays the form in Datasheet view, like the lower portion of the form in Figure 4-2.**

▶ **Multiple Items: Creates a form that lists each record in a continuously scrolling list.**

▶ **PivotChart: Creates a PivotChart grid in which you can drag-and-drop fields from the table to create various types of charts. Some people would argue that this is really not a form, but Access classifies it as one.**

▶ **Blank Form: Creates a blank layout grid into which you can manually add fields from tables and/or create other objects, such as navigation buttons. Beginners will not generally use this form creation option because it requires a deeper understanding of Form Design view than some other types.**

▶ **More Forms: Click this button for a menu of additional, less-common types.**

Creating a Form with the Form Wizard

One of the options on the More Forms button's menu is Form Wizard. This option walks you through a step-by-step process of creating a form. It is an easy, automated process, and yet it provides more choices than the automatically created forms you learned about in the previous section.

Follow these steps to use the Form Wizard:

1. Choose Create > Forms > More Forms > Form Wizard.

2. Open the Tables/Queries list and select the table or query on which the form should be based.

3. Select a field to include and click the > button, and repeat as needed. Or, click the >> button to quickly add all the fields. See Figure 4-3.

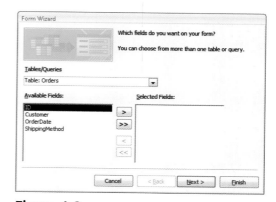

Figure 4-3
Select the data fields from one or more tables/queries.

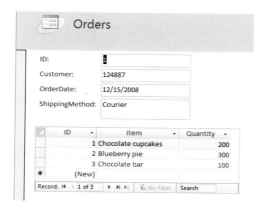

Figure 4-2
A form with a subform

4. (Optional) Repeat steps 2 and 3 to select fields from another table or query. If you select from more than one data source, Access will create a form/subform for you. The multiple data sources must have a relationship already established between them.

5. Click Next to continue.

6. If you chose fields from more than one table, you are asked whether you want a Form with Subform(s) or Linked Forms, and which form should be the main form. A linked form set places a button on one form that opens a related form for the other table. Make your choices, as in Figure 4-4, and click Next. (If you chose records from only one table, skip to step 8.)

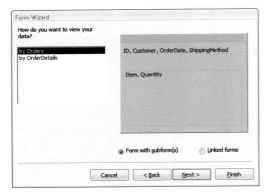

Figure 4-4
Choose which table should comprise the main form if you chose fields from more than one table.

7. If you are creating a form/subform, you are asked what type of subform layout you want. Datasheet is the default. Make your selection and click Next.

8. Select the formatting style for the form. See Figure 4-5. Then click Next.

Figure 4-5
Format a form using one of the preset formatting styles if desired.

9. Specify the name you want to use for the form. If you chose fields from more than one table, and chose to create a subform, you must also specify a name for the subform. See Figure 4-6.

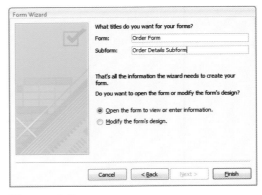

Figure 4-6
Name the form(s).

10. Click Finish. The form is created and saved.

Understanding Form Views

YOU CAN SWITCH VIEWS of a form by right-clicking its tab and clicking the desired view. You can also use the View button on the Home tab to choose from a menu of available views.

Each form has three possible views:

▶ **Form view**: Use this view to enter/edit data. This is the only view in which you can edit the records from the table/query on which the form is based. See Figure 4-7.

▶ **Layout view**: Use this view to modify the form's layout using an easy-to-manage layout grid. Not all types of formatting can be done from this view, but the formatting that is possible here is done quickly and easily. It is a what-you-see-is-what-you-get (WYSIWYG) view, providing a reliable picture of what the form will look like in Form view. See Figure 4-8.

▶ **Design view**: Use this view for precise control over every element of the form's design and layout. This view does not show the form exactly as it will appear in Form view, but it allows you to do things that you can't do in Layout view, like draw lines and shapes, import photos, and modify form headers and footers. Figure 4-9 shows Design view.

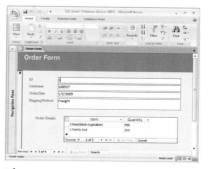

Figure 4-7
A form in Form view

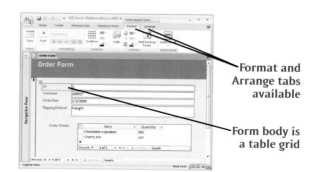

Format and Arrange tabs available

Form body is a table grid

Figure 4-8
A form in Layout view

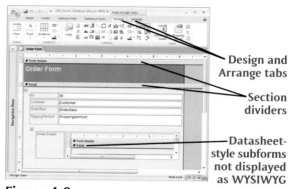

Design and Arrange tabs

Section dividers

Datasheet-style subforms not displayed as WYSIWYG

Figure 4-9
A form in Design view

Navigating Records in Form View

WITH THE DEFAULT FORM LAYOUT, only one record appears at a time. You can use the Record navigation controls at the bottom of the form to move between records. They are the same as the ones you learned about in Chapter 1 for datasheets. You can move forward and back between records or enter a specific record number. See Figure 4-10.

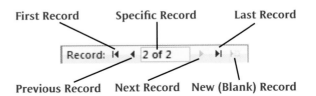

Figure 4-10
A form in Design view

Modifying a Form in Layout View

LAYOUT VIEW IS NEW IN Access 2007. It enables you to create and modify forms by dragging fields around on a grid in which the fields and labels automatically align neatly.

Adding and Removing Fields

Layout view makes it easy to add fields to the form because, in Layout view, all existing fields move to make room for the new field. Follow these steps:

1. In Design view, choose Design > Tools > Add Existing Fields. The Field List task pane appears.

2. Drag a field name from the Field List pane to the form, and drop it where you want it. See Figure 4-11.

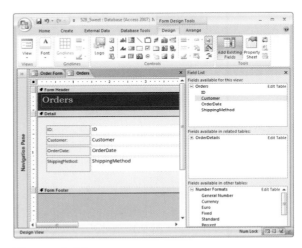

Figure 4-11
Drag fields from the Field List pane to the form.

To delete a field or other control, select it and press the Delete key. The field and its associated label are both deleted.

> If you want to delete only the label, leaving the field in place, you must perform the deletion in Design view.

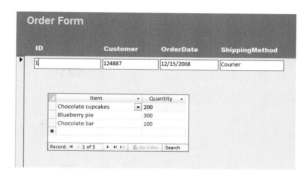

Figure 4-12
A form using Tabular layout

Moving Controls

To select a field or label in Layout view, click it. To select more than one, hold down Ctrl as you click each one. Then drag the selection to a new location to rearrange fields. When you move a label, its field moves with it, and vice versa.

> To select a block of fields, click the four-headed arrow icon in the upper left corner of that block. To deselect a block, click away from it.

> You can also break a field out of the layout so it can be dragged freely anywhere on the form. To do so, select it, and choose **Arrange > Control Layout > Remove.**

You can switch between them in Layout view by selecting all the fields, and then choosing Arrange > Control Layout > Tabular or Arrange > Control Layout > Stacked.

Switching Layouts

You can also change the layout of the fields on the form. There are two possible layouts: Stacked and Tabular. The Stacked layout is the default. It shows a field and label on a row, and the next field and label on the next row, and so on, as shown in Figures 4-8 and 4-9. The Tabular layout is more like a spreadsheet, where field names appear across the top and the fields themselves appear beneath the names. See Figure 4-12.

Resizing Controls

You can manually resize a control by dragging its border. Position the mouse pointer over the border so that the pointer becomes a double-headed arrow, and then drag. You can also auto-size a control to fit the entry in it. To do so, select the control and then choose Arrange > Size > Size to Fit.

Formatting Controls

When a control on a form is selected, you can use the options on the Format tab (see Figure 4-13):

- ▶ **Change the item's font or font size.**
- ▶ **Change whether the text is bold, italic, or underlined.**
- ▶ **Choose left-aligned, centered, or right-aligned.**
- ▶ **Choose the color of the background, text, and border.**
- ▶ **Choose the style and width of the line or of the border surrounding the box.**

You can also use the text formatting options on the Home tab while in Layout view. Many of them duplicate those on the Format tab.

All of the preceding formatting features work just as they do in other Microsoft Office programs that you might already be familiar with. If you make an error while formatting, click the Undo button on the Quick Access toolbar immediately after a change.

Adding a Title

Depending on how you created the form, it may or may not already have a title. A title is a text label that appears at the top of the form, explaining what it is for. For example, in Figure 4-12, the title is Order Form.

To add a title to the form from Layout view, choose Format > Controls > Title. This creates a placeholder text label at the top of the form (in its header area). You can then replace the dummy text with your own wording.

If the form already has a title, clicking the Title button inserts another title placeholder, which might appear over the top of the existing one. You probably don't want two titles, so delete one of them.

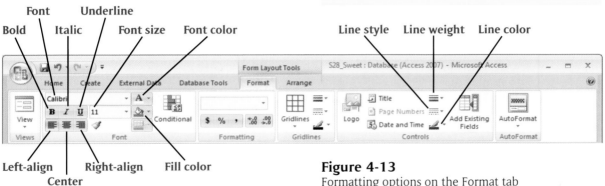

Figure 4-13
Formatting options on the Format tab

Adding a Logo

A logo is a small picture. You might want to place your company's logo on each form, for example. To place a logo on the form from Layout view, follow these steps:

1. Choose Format > Controls > Logo. The Insert Picture dialog box opens.

2. Select the picture to use as the logo. See Figure 4-14.

3. Click OK. The logo appears in a small box in the top-left corner of the form. You can drag it to another location if desired.

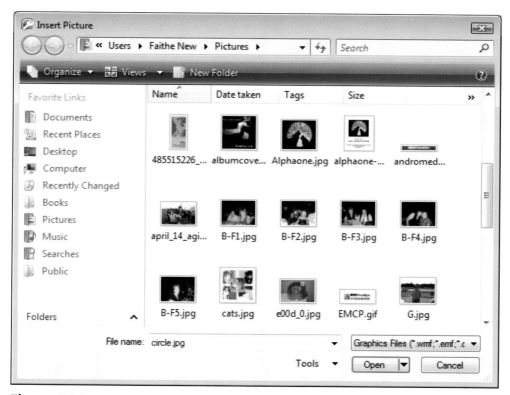

Figure 4-14
Select a picture to use as the logo on the form.

Editing a Form in Design View

DESIGN VIEW FOR A FORM consists of a blank slate on which you place fields, labels, and other controls. You can drag them around freely. Design view provides the most flexibility in creating the exact look and feel you want for your form, but it does so at the expense of convenience. Controls do not automatically align with one another, for example, and when you delete and add controls, the others do not move automatically to accommodate the change.

You can do almost everything in Design view that you can do in Layout view, plus you can add other controls such as drop-down lists, check boxes, charts, and lines. You can place codes on the form that display the date and time, record or page numbers, and other information by using functions similar to those in Excel. You can also fine-tune the placement of items more precisely, as well as move and delete labels separately from their fields and vice versa.

If you created the form in Layout view or with the Form Wizard, the fields are in a Stacked or Tabular layout. This doesn't change in Design view. However, if the form was upgraded from a previous version of Access or manually created in Design view by dragging fields into the grid, the fields are free-floating. Fields behave differently, depending on whether they are free-floating. You can move fields in or out of a layout with the Tabular, Stacked, and Remove buttons on the Arrange tab.

Selecting and Moving Controls

When you click a control that is part of a layout, an orange border appears around it, just as in Layout view. Dragging a field also moves the associated label; they cannot be separated.

When you click a control that is free-floating (not part of a layout), the field and its associated label each have a brown square in the upper-left corner. You can drag it by its square to move one piece separately from the other. This is how you would move a label separately from its text box, for example. See Figure 4-15. If you need to work with a label separately from its field, but it is part of a Stacked or Tabular layout, select that individual field and choose Arrange > Control Layout > Remove.

Figure 4-15
A free-floating control has a brown square that can be used as a handle for moving it.

It is often easier to remove all the fields/labels from the layout than to just do one because if you remove just one field, the remaining fields in the layout grid may overlap it, making it hard to select and work with.

Resizing Controls

When a field is part of a layout, resizing options for it are limited. You can resize it horizontally by dragging its right edge, but this also resizes all other fields in that column by an equal amount.

However, when the control is broken out of the layout, it has a full set of selection handles on all sides and can be resized individually in any direction by dragging any of these.

Working with Headers and Footers

Headers and footers on a form provide a place to enter objects that relate to the entire form rather than to an individual record. They are managed from Design view. Forms that you create via the Form Wizard or the Form button automatically have a form header set up. Forms that you build manually do not.

Onscreen, headers and footers appear at the top and bottom of a form, providing information. For example, if you create a form title, as you learned earlier in this chapter, it appears in the Form Header area. See Figure 4-16.

To display or hide the form Header/Footer areas, choose Arrange > Show/Hide > Form Header/Footer. See Figure 4-16.

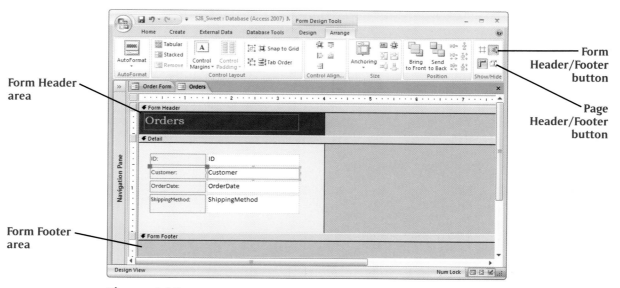

Figure 4-16
The title label (Orders) appears in the Form Header area.

You might notice in Figure 4-16 that there is also a Page Header/Footer button. Page headers/footers are not commonly used on forms, but they are common on reports (which share a common set of controls in Design view with forms). Whatever you enter in the page header or footer appears in each page of a multipage form or printout. You might place a page numbering code there, for example. The page header and footer print at the top or bottom of the page but do not display in Form view.

Changing the Height of a Form Section

Each section of the form (Form Header, Detail, Form Footer) is resizable. You can drag the bar at the bottom of each section up or down to increase or decrease the above section's size. For example, to change the size of the Form Header area, drag the Detail bar up or down.

Notice in Figure 4-15 that the Form Footer area is not only blank, but has zero height. This is to avoid it taking up space onscreen unnecessarily. If you wanted to put something in the form footer, you could position the mouse pointer below the Form Footer section title and drag down to increase the size of the footer area.

Adding a Date or Time Code

You can add a date and/or time code to the form. It will appear in Form view and also when you print the form. The date/time is updated from the computer's internal clock. To get started, choose Design > Controls > Date & Time.

The Date and Time dialog box appears. You can choose to include the date, the time, or both with the respective check boxes. You can also choose among three formats for each. See Figure 4-17. A date/time code is always placed in the form header; you cannot choose where to insert it. You can, however, move it to another section, such as the Form Footer area, after its insertion. (See the next section.)

Moving Controls Between Sections

You cannot drag-and-drop controls between sections. However, you can use the Cut and Paste commands. For example, to move a date/time code from the form header to the form footer, select it, press Ctrl+X to cut it to the Clipboard, and then select the Form Footer selection bar and press Ctrl+V to paste it into that section.

Figure 4-17
Insert a date or time code.

If you insert a date or time code but you can't see it, and your form header has a dark background color, it is probably there but just obscured by the similarity of its text color to the background color.

Creating Simple
Queries

SOMETIMES WHEN FACED with a mountain of data, it can be difficult to see the meaning. Picture yourself faced with a large table of data and being asked to pick out certain facts from it, such as the customer who bought the highest quantity of a particular item or the date on which a sales quota was met.

Queries can help you find that meaning in a wide variety of ways. A query can show you a subset of data from a table, such as only certain records or only certain fields. It can combine fields from multiple tables, and it can create calculated fields on the fly, such as calculating a total cost by multiplying data from a unit price field by data from a quantity field. Queries can also present data in a certain order that is different from the order in the underlying table.

In this chapter, you'll start your journey with queries by creating some simple ones that present certain fields from one or more tables. Then in the following chapter you'll expand that knowledge by learning how to filter and summarize with queries.

Creating Queries

QUERY IS A VIEW OF the data from one or more tables. That view can be altered in perspective from the original in a variety of ways. For example, the query might show the data in a different sort order, or with fewer fields shown, or fewer records based on some criteria you specify.

Queries are useful in creating subsets of fields that make it simpler to look up data. For example, suppose you have a table of customer information that contains 50 fields, but most of the time you are looking up a few specific points of information, such as the customer's ZIP code or ID number. A query can present a simplified version of the table's datasheet with just the most popular fields, making it a much easier browse.

A query is not just a convenience tool, though; queries can do things that tables cannot do at all. Let's say, for example, that you want to see what products each customer has been ordering. Customer information is stored in one table, order summaries in another, and the detail about the items ordered in yet another. You would have to jump around to three different tables to collect the data you needed. Queries come to the rescue here by enabling you to combine data from multiple tables into a single datasheet. You can then use that query as the basis for a form, report, or another query.

Using the Query Wizard

The Query Wizard provides a simple step-by-step walkthrough of the query creation process. It enables you to select fields from one or more tables for inclusion.

> **The Query Wizard does not allow you to set up criteria for showing a subset of the records. You will learn how to manually set up criteria in Chapter 6.**

For a single-table query, follow these steps:

1. Choose Create > Other > Query Wizard. The New Query dialog box opens.

2. Click Simple Query Wizard and click OK. The Simple Query Wizard opens.

3. Open the Tables/Queries drop-down list and select the table.

4. Click a field to include on the Available Fields list, and click the > button to move it to the Selected Fields list. Repeat as needed for other fields, or to include all fields, click >>. See Figure 5-1.

5. Repeat steps 3 and 4 as needed to select fields from other related tables. Then click Next.

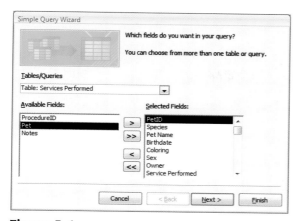

Figure 5-1
Select the fields to include in the query.

The query you just created is not very feature-rich; it is basically just a datasheet that includes fields you specify from one or more tables. You will learn how to make more interesting queries that do more useful things later in this chapter and in Chapter 6.

Examining a Query in Design View

Before we move on to creating a query from scratch, let's have a look at the query you just created. To open it in Design view, do any of the following:

▶ **If the query is open in Datasheet view, right-click its tab and choose Design View.**

▶ **If the query is open in Datasheet view, choose Home > Views > View. The button that appears at the top is for Design view, so clicking it takes you directly to Design view; alternatively you can click the down arrow at the bottom of the button to open a menu and choose Design View from that menu.**

▶ **Right-click the query's name in the Navigation pane and click Design View.**

In Design view, the tables you chose when you created the query appear as field lists in the upper pane. The lower pane shows the fields you chose, one per column. Figure 5-3 shows an example.

6. If you are asked whether you want a detail or summary query, choose Detail. See Figure 5-2. Click Next.

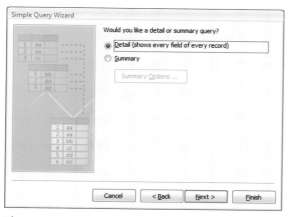

Figure 5-2
Choose a detail query if prompted.

7. Change the query title if desired in the What Title Do You Want for Your Query? text box.

8. Click Finish. The query results open in Datasheet view.

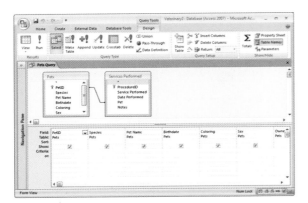

Figure 5-3
A query in Design view

Notice in Figure 5-3 that the tables have a relationship line between them. This relationship was created in the Relationships window using the procedure outlined in Chapter 3; it transfers automatically to the query when the two tables are both included in the query's design.

Here's an explanation of each of the rows in the lower portion of Figure 5-3:

- ▶ **Field**: Lists the field name.

- ▶ **Table**: Lists the table from which that field comes. This is automatically filled in for you. Unless you are working with two tables that have fields with identical names, this should not be an issue.

- ▶ **Sort**: If you set up the query to sort by a particular field, Ascending or Descending appears in this row for that field. Sorting is covered later in this chapter.

- ▶ **Show**: When the check box is marked, that field will appear in the query result datasheet; clear the check box to hide that field from the results. This is necessary because sometimes you have to include a query for calculation purposes that you don't need to see in the datasheet. You'll see an example of this later in the chapter, when we look at creating calculated fields.

- ▶ **Criteria**: This is where you would enter the specifications for any record filtering you wanted to do. Chapter 6 explains how to do this.

- ▶ **Or**: This line enables you to have multiple criteria. Again, this is explained in Chapter 6.

Creating a New Query in Design View

Now that you have a general idea of what Design view for a query entails, let's create a query from scratch.

Follow these steps to create a query in Design view:

1. Choose Create > Other > Query Design. The Show Table dialog box opens.

2. Click a table or query to use and click Add. (Alternatively, you can double-click the table or query name.) Repeat to add more if needed, then click Close. See Figure 5-4.

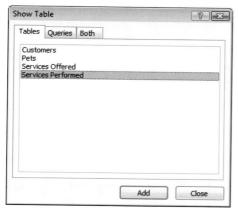

Figure 5-4
Select the tables from which the query's fields will come.

3. Drag a field from one of the tables into the first empty column in the lower pane. Alternatively you can double-click the field name to place it in the lower pane.

4. Repeat step 3 to add more fields. Figure 5-5 shows a query with fields from several tables.

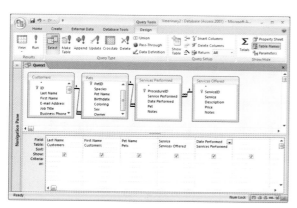

Figure 5-5
Drag fields from the lists into the query design grid at the bottom.

Fields will appear in the datasheet in the order they appear in the lower pane of Design view. You can rearrange the fields at any time. Select a column by clicking the thin gray bar above it, and then drag it to the right or left to move it.

5. To check your work, choose Design > Results > View. Then to get back to Design view, from the datasheet choose Home > Views > View.

6. Click the Save button on the Quick Access toolbar to save your query. In the Save As dialog box, type the name for the query and click OK. See Figure 5-6.

Figure 5-6
Save the query design.

Modifying a Query in Design View

NOW THAT YOU HAVE seen how to create a query, let's look at how to modify one. As you have already seen in this chapter, you can open any query in Design view, regardless of the method of its creation. From there you can use the various properties in the rows of the lower grid to specify how each field should appear.

Sorting Data in a Query

The Sort row in the query design grid enables you to sort the query results by one or more fields. Click in the Sort row for a field's column, and then open the drop-down list there and choose Ascending (which is A to Z) or Descending (which is Z to A). See Figure 5-7.

Figure 5-7
Choose a field by which to sort the results.

If you choose more than one field for sorting, Access sorts the results first by the leftmost column that is set for sorting. It uses the additional field for sorting only in the event of a tie in the primary sort column.

Suppose you want the primary sort field to be a field that appears to the right of the secondary sort field in the query results. If you do not want to reorder the fields in the query results, here is a workaround. Place an extra copy of the primary sort field in the leftmost field position, and clear the Show check box for it so that it does not appear in the query results. Then set it for Ascending or Descending sort.

Creating a Calculated Field

One of the benefits of a query is that you can create additional fields on the fly—fields that do not exist in any table. The fields appear in the query results datasheet, looking just as if they were actual fields from a table. This is great because you can use the values in other fields to generate useful information without having to keep that information stored permanently.

For example, suppose your company has standard prices for each service it offers, and your boss has asked you to recalculate what the prices would be if you increased them by 10% across the board. He doesn't actually want to raise the prices yet; he just wants the what-if information. You could create a query that includes a calculated field to figure that out.

Suppose that the current prices are in a field called Price. You could write the following formula to calculate the 10% increase:

```
[Price]*1.1
```

To create a calculated field, follow these steps from Design view:

1. Click in the Field row in a blank column, and type the name you want for the column heading on the calculated field.

2. Type a colon (:).

3. Type the formula that will perform the calculation. Enclose field names in square brackets, and use the following standard math operators:

   + Addition

   − Subtraction

   * Multiplication

   / Division

4. Switch to Datasheet view to check your results. Then switch back to Design view. Figure 5-8 shows the example mentioned earlier, where the price is being increased by 10% and presented in a column called New Price. Table 5-1 shows some examples of calculated fields.

Figure 5-8
Create a calculated field.

Table 5-1 Calculated Fields

To Do the Following:	Example of Calculated Field Code
Multiply UnitPrice by Quantity	Total:[UnitPrice]*[Quantity]
Decrease the UnitPrice by $10	Discount Price:[UnitPrice]−10
Decrease the UnitPrice by the value in the Discount field	Discount Price:[UnitPrice]−[Discount]

Concatenating Fields

Concatenation is a special type of calculation. It enables you to combine text strings from multiple fields in a single column in the query results. For example, suppose you store the customers' first and last names in separate fields, but in the query results you want to show the customers' full names in a single column. Concatenation can do that.

To create a concatenated field, use the & operator. To include a space between the concatenated fields, use a space enclosed in quotation marks, like this: " ". So, to combine the First Name and Last Name fields into a single column called Name, you might create a calculated field like this:

```
Name:[First Name]&" "&[Last Name]
```

Changing the Caption for a Field

In the last two sections, you saw how you can specify the column heading by putting the desired text in front of the formula, separated by a colon. You can do this for any field, not just the calculated fields. For example, suppose you are using a Pet Name field in the query, and you want it to appear as Pet in the query results. You could type **Pet:** in front of the field name in the Field row to achieve this. See Figure 5-9.

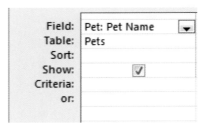

Figure 5-9
Caption a field by typing the caption and a colon to the left of the field name.

Creating Queries that Filter and

Summarize Data

THE REAL POWER OF A QUERY comes from its ability to drill down through large quantities of data to locate what you need, whether that is a specific set of records that match certain criteria or a broad-picture summary that tells you something about the aggregate, such as a count of the number of customers in a certain category or a total of the dollar value of sales in a certain month.

In this chapter, you'll continue your work with queries, learning how to create filter criteria that can weed out extraneous records to show only the records of interest to answer a particular question. You will also learn how to create summary queries that give you a high-level view of your data and parameter queries that prompt you for information on the fly each time you run the query.

Creating a Query that Shows Only Certain Records

To FILTER THE RESULTS OF YOUR query, place criteria statements in the Criteria row for each field that is involved in the filter. For example, you might enter a specific ZIP code in the ZIP Code field to limit the query results to only customers who live in that ZIP code area.

There are many types of criteria statements you can use, depending on what results you want. The following sections each address a specific type of criteria.

Filtering for Exact Values

Exact value criteria are very easy to create; you simply type the desired value directly into the Criteria row for that field. The query results will show only records where that field exactly matches the value you entered.

Simply entering the criteria bare like that will not match partial values. For example, if you enter VAC as the criterion for the Service field, it will not include records where the Service field's entry is VACS or OVAC. (If you need that kind of matching, see the next section.)

For logical Yes/No fields, you will almost always use exact values for your criteria because there are only two possible values. For example, to find records when the Married? field is set to Yes, enter Yes in the Criteria row for that field.

Depending on the data type, Access may modify the Criteria entry in some way. For example, if you enter a text string, it puts quotation marks around it for you. You can enter the quotation marks yourself if you like, but it is not necessary. And if you enter a date, it encloses it in pound (#) marks.

Filtering for Pattern Matches

If you need to match a part of a field and not the entire field, then you need a pattern match, aka a **wildcard match**. With this type of criterion, you specify a partial value, and then you use the following wildcard characters to allow multiple values within that pattern: the asterisk (*) to refer to any number of characters or the question mark (?) to refer to a single character.

Pattern match criteria always begin with the word *Like*. So, for example, to find all records in which the Service field's entry begins with the letter V, you would enter:

```
Like "V*"
```

Notice that the * character is inside the quotation marks; that is important. Notice also that even though the word Like is text, it is not in the quotation marks because it is an instruction.

You can put the * or ? symbol either at the beginning or the end of the text string, and you can use as many ? signs as you like, each standing for one character. Table 6-1 shows some examples.

Filtering with Conditional (Boolean) Expressions

Another way to filter records is by creating a **conditional expression** that compares the records' values to a Boolean statement.

(A **Boolean statement** is a logical expression that results in a yes/no answer and is named after George Boole, a famous mathematician.) For example, you might want dates that are earlier than a certain date you specify or quantities that are below a certain value. To create these statements, you use **comparison operators**. Table 6-2 lists the comparison operators that Access allows in a query and examples of them.

Table 6-1 Examples of Pattern-Match Criteria

Example	Finds This	Would Include	Would Not Include
Like "?A*"	Entries where the second letter in the text string is A	Water, Aardvark, PA	American, Persia
Like "????"	Entries with exactly four characters	Bone, Seat, Arts	Bones, Sea, Ankle
Like "*S"	Entries that end in S	Bones, Seas	Sank, Desk
Like "13.*"	Entries that are the number 13, regardless of any decimal places	13, 13.16, 13.9987	12.3, 100

Table 6-2 Comparison Operators

Operator	Meaning	Example	Would Include	Would Not Include
>	Greater than	>100	101, 200	−101, −100, 0, 100
<	Less than	<100	−101, −100, 0, 100	101, 200
>=	Greater than or equal to	>=100	100, 101, 200	−101, −100, 0, 99
<=	Less than or equal to	<=100	−101, −100, 0, 99	100, 101, 200
=	Equal to	=100	100	Anything except 100
< >	Not equal to	< >100	Anything except 100	100

When you use comparison operators with text strings (which is not common), it evaluates them alphabetically. For example, >"C*" would find text strings that begin with the letters C through Z but not strings that begin with A or B.

When you use comparison operators with dates, it evaluates them chronologically. For example, <=#01/01/09# finds dates that are before or equal to January 1, 2009.

You can combine multiple expressions in a single statement by using logical operators such as AND and OR. Table 6-3 lists the logical operators that Access accepts for queries. In Table 6-3, assume that Exp1 and Exp2 are two separate expressions that you would combine with a logical operator. For example, >100 AND <200 would find all values between 101 and 199, inclusive. Operators are not case-sensitive.

Table 6-3 Logical Operators

Operator	Returns "True" When . . .
AND	Both Exp1 and Exp2 must be true.
OR	Either Exp1 or Exp2 must be true.
EQV	The true/false values of both expressions are the same. So, either Exp1 and Exp2 are both true, or Exp1 and Exp2 are both false.
NOT	The expression is not true (used with only a single expression, Exp1).
XOR	One of the expressions is true, but not both of them. So, either Exp1 is true and Exp2 is false, or vice versa.

Another way to create multiple criteria, as an alternative to the OR operator, is to enter the additional expression in the OR line of the query design grid.

Filtering for Null or Non-Null Values

To find (or avoid finding) records where a certain field is blank, use the IS NULL or IS NOT NULL operator in the Criteria row. For example, IS NULL in the City field would find all records for which you had not yet entered a value in that field.

Filtering for a Range

To specify a range of values, use the BETWEEN operator. For example, to find dates between 01/01/2009 and 01/01/2010, you could enter BETWEEN #01/01/09# AND #01/01/10#. The results from a BETWEEN expression are inclusive, so in this example, the dates January 1, 2009 and January 1, 2010 would both be included.

Filtering with a List of Values

Sometimes you might want to filter for multiple specific values. For example, if looking for customers from the Midwest, you might filter for certain states in the State field including IN, IL, OH, MI, and IA. Some ways to look for any of a list of values would be to use multiple OR lines in the query design grid, or multiple OR operators in a Boolean statement. However, there is an easier way than those: use the IN function. To use the IN function, type **IN**, and then in parentheses after it, type the values, separated by commas. If they are text strings, put them in quotes. (Do not use quotes for numeric values.) For example:

```
IN("Red","Green","Blue")
IN(1, 10, 20, 50)
```

Prompting the User for a Parameter

I F YOU WANT TO FILTER on a certain value, but that value varies, you might find yourself creating lots of queries. For example, suppose you want to filter a list of customers according to the state they live in. There are 50 states, so you would need 50 queries to be able to filter by any one state on demand.

For situations like that, it is better to create a **parameter query**. They enable you to use the same query to extract data according to a criterion that you enter each time the query runs. Parameter query results can also be the source for a report or form. For example, you could run a query that extracts all the customers who live in Illinois, and then use those results as a data source for printing mailing labels.

Prompting from the Criteria Row

The most common type of parameter occurs in the Criteria row of a query. Place the message you want for the prompt in square brackets. For example, if you want the user to enter a state, you might use [Which state?].

> If the user needs any special instructions to make the query work right, put them in the bracketed prompt. For example, if you want them to enter a two-character state code, and not the state name, you might use [Please enter the two-character state abbreviation:].

When you run the query (by switching to Datasheet view or choosing Design > Results > Run), your prompt appears in a dialog box, along with a blank text box for user input. See Figure 6-1.

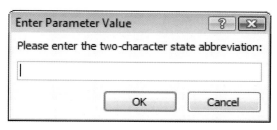

Figure 6-1
Dialog box from the criteria parameter

Access takes the value typed in the text box and places it in the Criteria row in place of the prompt to select the records.

> **If you want to rerun the prompt from Datasheet view without returning to Design view, you can press Shift+F9.**

The prompt can be combined with other criteria to permit a variety of responses. Suppose, again, that you were prompting for a particular state. Table 6-4 shows some entries and what results they would produce.

Table 6-4 Parameter Examples

Entry in Criteria Row	Result
`[Which State?]`	Only exact matches are found.
`Like [Which State?]`	Any portion of the field content can be specified with a wildcard. For example, if the user enters C*, the query results include CA, CO, and CN; if the user enters *A, the results include CA, IA, PA, and WA.
`Like [Which State?] & "*"`	If the user enters nothing, all records show. If the user enters any character, it finds records that contain that character in any position.

Prompting from the Field Row

You can also place a parameter in the Field row. Generally, the purpose of a field parameter is to allow the user to enter a variable for a calculated field on the fly each time the query runs.

For example, you may want to see the value of a variable price increase for every item you sell. Suppose that Retail Price is the name of the field containing the prices. You might enter the following in a new column in the query design grid:

```
New Price:[Retail Price]*[Percentage of Increase]
```

New Price is the caption you are assigning to the calculated field. [Retail Price] is the field name. And [Percentage of Increase] is the prompt for the variable. When you run the query, Access displays a dialog box with the prompt Percentage of Increase.

The preceding example is a bit oversimplified, though, because the user is likely to enter a whole number in response to that prompt. In other words, if asked for a percentage of increase, the user might type 10, meaning 10%. However multiplying the retail price by 10 would result in a 1000% increase, not a 10% increase. Therefore, you need to divide the number entered by 100, and then add it to the original retail price, like this:

```
New Price:(([Retail Price]*[Percentage of
Increase])/100)*[Retail Price]
```

These results do not permanently affect the data in the table; they merely provide a calculation that exists within the query results only.

> **If you want to permanently change the values in the table, you could use an Update query. Update queries are not covered in this book, but you can find out more about them in the Help system in Access.**

Managing Multiple Prompts

You can type multiple prompts in one query or even in one box within the query. For example, if you have an invoice date, you could type

```
Between [Enter Start Date:] and [Enter End Date:]
```

to create two prompts to give you a date range to select specific invoices within a date range.

If you have multiple parameters in the query, the order of the prompts might not be to your liking. If so, you can use the Query Parameters dialog box to set up the order in which Access prompts the user.

Follow these steps to change the prompt order:

1. Choose Design > Show/Hide > Parameters.

2. Type (or copy) the parameters exactly as you have them in the Criteria or Field row in the order you want them to execute. The order of the prompts in the dialog box becomes the order in which the user will be prompted. See Figure 6-2.

If you do not have the parameter identical (including punctuation and spacing) in the query design grid and the Query Parameters dialog box, you will get two prompts.

3. (Optional) If desired, set a data type for each parameter. Access will notify the user if the data entered in the prompt is not of the appropriate type.

4. Click OK.

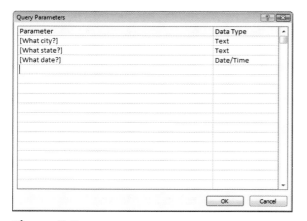

Figure 6-2
Set up the parameters in the order in which they should execute.

Creating a Summary Query

A SUMMARY QUERY IS VERY different in purpose from a detail (normal) query. It usually does not contain very many fields—only the fields that you are interested in either grouping by or calculating some statistic about.

Whereas a detail query shows every record that matches the query criteria, a summary query just shows a statistical summary. This can be very useful when trying to make strategic business decisions from a large quantity of data.

Using the Simple Query Wizard to Summarize

When you create a query that contains numeric data fields, the Simple Query Wizard gives you the option of either a detail or summary query, as you saw in Chapter 5. In that chapter, we used the Detail query option. If you choose Summary, you can select one or more aggregate functions. An **aggregate function** is one that summarizes the data by performing a certain math calculation such as Average, Sum, or Count.

Follow these steps to create a summary query with the Simple Query Wizard:

1. Choose Create > Other > Query Wizard.

2. Click Simple Query Wizard, and click OK.

3. Select the fields from which to create the query, from one or more existing tables or queries, just as you learned in Chapter 5. Make sure that at least one of the fields contains numeric data. See Figure 6-3. Then click Next.

> For a summary query, be very selective about which fields you include. If you are not going to group by a field or summarize it with an aggregate function, do not include it.

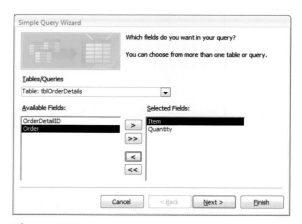

Figure 6-3
Select the fields to include.

4. Click Summary. The Summary Options button becomes available.

5. Click Summary Options. The Summary Options dialog box opens.

6. Click to place a check mark for each aggregate function you want for each field. See Figure 6-4.

7. (Optional) If you want a record count, mark the Count Records In check box.

8. Click OK to close the Summary Options dialog box. Then click Next to continue.

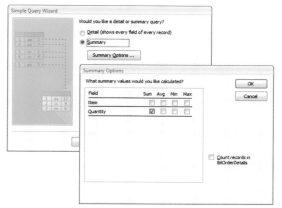

Figure 6-4
Set up the aggregate functions for the summary query.

9. If prompted, choose how you want the values grouped, and then click Next. This step appears only if you have chosen a field with a groupable type, such as date (which can be grouped into Month, Year, and so on).

10. If desired, change the query name in the What Title Do You Want for Your Query? box.

11. Click Finish. The query results appear in a datasheet.

Notice that in the datasheet, the column name for the summary reflects the aggregate function you chose. For example, in Figure 6-5, the column heading Sum of Quantity reflects that I chose to apply the Sum aggregate function to the Quantity field.

Item	Sum Of Quantity
Votive mold, square	6
Pillar mold 9"x3"	1
Mold sealant	1
Votive/pillar wax, 10lb	3
Container wax, 10lb	6
Stearic acid	4
Vybar 103	2
Tealight candle	12
Tealight candle	12
6" zinc votive wicks	21
4" zinc tealight wicks	2

Figure 6-5
The query results appear in Datasheet view.

The Simple Query Wizard has many advantages over the manual method you will learn about later for creating a summary query, including the ability to group data in chunks (such as for a whole month of dates together rather than each individual date separately) without writing the complex code required for it manually.

For a look at the underpinnings of the query, switch over to Design view. Figure 6-6 shows an example. Notice that a Total row appears in the query design grid; you haven't seen this row in any other queries we've worked with so far. Notice also on the Design tab that the Totals button is selected. This button toggles the Totals row on and off.

Each field must have an entry in the Total row. The default entry is Group By, which means that field will define individual rows in the summary datasheet. Look again at Figure 6-5, and notice that each unique item name appears as a row.

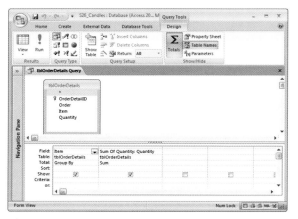

Figure 6-6
A summary query created with the Simple Query Wizard, in Design view.

Then look again at Figure 6-6 and see that the Item field is set for Group By.

If a field is not grouped by, in a summary query, then it is calculated. Notice in Figure 6-6 that the Total row for the Quantity field shows Sum. Then look back at Figure 6-5 and see that the Sum of Quantity column summarizes the quantity of each of the items across all orders that were placed.

Creating a Summary Query in Design View

As an alternative to the Simple Query Wizard method, you can create a summary query on your own in Design view. This might be useful if you want to copy a preexisting detail query and set up the copy as a summary query, for example, or if you know exactly what you want and don't want to work through the wizard to get there.

To turn any query into a summary query, choose Design > Show/Hide > Totals. Then choose Group By or one of the functions from the Total row's drop-down list for each field. See Figure 6-7.

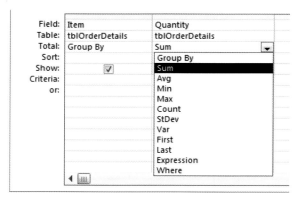

Figure 6-7
Choose how you want the query summarized and grouped.

> If you summarize a field using a selection from the Totals row manually, the field caption does not change to reflect the chosen aggregate function the way it does when you use the wizard method. Therefore, you might want to change the field caption yourself, as you learned in Chapter 5, by typing a caption and a colon to the left of the field name in the Field row.

7

Creating

Reports

PICTURE A BUSINESS EXECUTIVE in another branch of your company, in a high-level planning meeting that will dictate the company's future. A question arises about the company's product line, and someone pulls out a printed report that was generated—from your database—that answers the question. The neatly formatted report is easy to read and understand, and it provides just the information that is needed in that moment.

Many of the people who will benefit from the databases you create in Access will never use the database directly. They will instead receive printed or e-mailed reports containing information that will help them make business decisions. These reports may contain either more or less information than the underlying tables do, and may arrange and present the data as a summary or as a detailed log of every item.

In this chapter, you will learn how to create simple yet effective reports in Access, suitable for printing. You'll learn how to print a report, how to set print options such as margins, and how to prepare reports suitable for e-mail distribution.

Understanding Reports

WHILE YOU CAN PRINT tables, queries, and forms whenever needed, it is often better to create a **report** when you need a printout. Reports present data in a format optimized for printing. Reports share some characteristics of both forms and queries. Like a form, a report is a user-friendly window on one or more tables, and Report Design view is very similar to Form Design view in terms of its interface and capabilities. Like a query, a report can contain special-purpose fields generated specifically for it, such as aggregate functions. Reports can also sort and group records by any criteria you specify.

There are four main types of report layouts.

▶ In a tabular report, each row is a record and each column is a field. It's similar to the printout you get when printing a datasheet. See Figure 7-1.

▶ In a columnar report, all the fields for each record appear together, followed by those for the next record, and so on. It's similar to the printout you get when printing a form. See Figure 7-2.

▶ In a justified report, the field names appear above the fields for each individual record, arranged in blocks. See Figure 7-3.

▶ In a mailing label report, records are arranged in blocks across and down the page, ready to print on a sheet of self-stick labels.

Tabular Report

Last Name	First Name	Job Title	Business Phone
Bedecs	Anna	Owner	(123)555-0100
Gratacos S‹	Antonio	Owner	(123)555-0100
Axen	Thomas	Purchasing Representative	(123)555-0100
Lee	Christina	Purchasing Manager	(123)555-0100
O'Donnell	Martin	Owner	(123)555-0100
Pérez-Olae	Francisco	Purchasing Manager	(123)555-0100
Xie	Ming-Yang	Owner	(123)555-0100
Andersen	Elizabeth	Purchasing Representative	(123)555-0100
Mortensen	Sven	Purchasing Manager	(123)555-0100
Wacker	Roland	Purchasing Manager	(123)555-0100

Figure 7-1
A tabular report

Columnar Report

Last Name	Bedecs
First Name	Anna
E-mail Address	
Job Title	Owner
Business Phone	(123)555-0100

Last Name	Gratacos Solsona
First Name	Antonio
E-mail Address	
Job Title	Owner
Business Phone	(123)555-0100

Figure 7-2
A columnar report

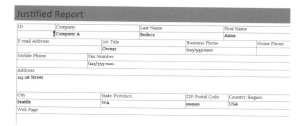

Figure 7-3
A justified report

The Views buttons in the bottom right corner of the report window enable you to quickly switch between views. See Figure 7-4. You can also switch views by choosing Design > Views or Home > Views and selecting from the menu of views. (The Design tab is available only if you are in Design view.)

Views for Working with Reports

There are four views for working with reports:

▶ **Design**: Uses a grid to precisely arrange fields and other controls; enables you to add non-field controls like formulas and labels. The layout does not look exactly as it will when printed, so you must switch between this view and others to check your work.

▶ **Layout**: Shows the report approximately as it will look when printed and is editable. You can add and remove fields, resize controls, and so on.

▶ **Report**: Shows the report optimized for onscreen viewing. The report is not editable in this view.

▶ **Print Preview**: Shows the report exactly as it will look when printed. The report is not editable in this view. Print Preview and Report views are very similar.

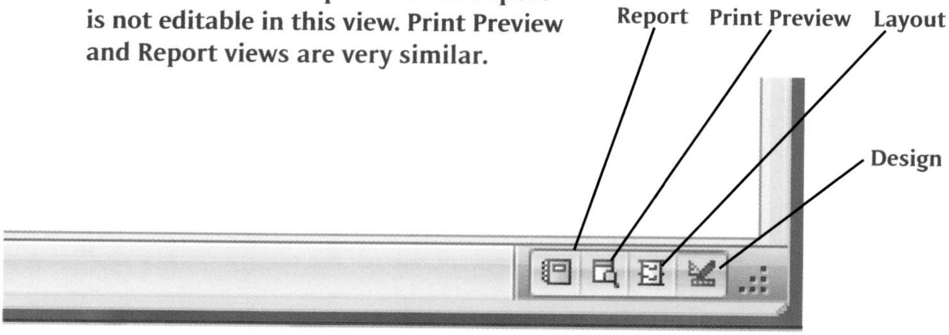

Report   Print Preview   Layout

Design

Figure 7-4
The Views buttons for reports

Creating a Simple Report

THERE ARE SEVERAL METHODS of creating a report:

▶ You can choose Create > Reports > Report. This creates a tabular report from the selected object and opens it in Layout view.

▶ You can choose Create > Reports > Blank Report. This starts a blank report in Layout view, onto which you can drag fields from a list.

▶ You can choose Create > Reports > Report Wizard to run a wizard that walks you step by step through the process.

▶ You can choose Create > Reports > Report Design to create a new report in Design view, which is similar to Design view for a form.

▶ You can choose Create > Reports > Labels to use the Label Wizard, which walks you step by step through creating a label report.

You can also copy an existing report and make changes to it.

Creating a Quick Tabular Report

To create a quick tabular report, display a datasheet on which you want to base the report (either a table or a query), and then choose Create > Reports > Report. The report opens in Layout view, as shown in Figure 7-5.

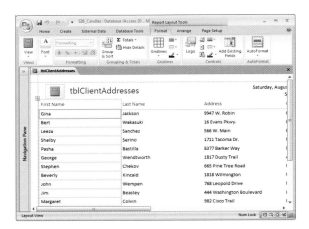

Figure 7-5
A tabular report in Layout view

The resulting report might not be exactly perfect —for example, the column widths might not be quite right, or the title might need changing— but it'll likely be at least in the ballpark, and then you can tweak it in Layout or Design view, as you will learn later in this chapter.

Creating a Report with the Report Wizard

The Report Wizard is similar to other wizards you have already seen in Access. It is a step-by-step guide to creating a report.

Follow these steps to create a report with the Report Wizard:

1. Choose Create > Reports > Report Wizard.

2. Select the fields to include in the report. You can choose from more than one table or query. This works just the same as in the Query Wizard and Form Wizard. See Figure 7-6. Then click Next.

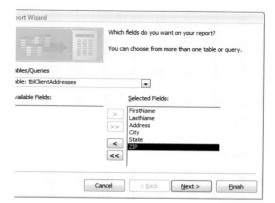

Figure 7-6
Select the fields for the report.

3. If you want the report grouped by a certain field, select it and click > to move it to the sample as a group heading. See Figure 7-7. Then click Next.

Figure 7-7
Choose a field by which to group, if desired.

You can group by more than one field. This results in groups within groups. For example, you might group by State, and then within each state you might group by City. If grouping by multiple fields, make sure you select them in order of precedence. (For example, select State first, then City.)

4. If you want the records sorted by a certain field within the groups, open the 1 drop-down list and select the field. See Figure 7-8.

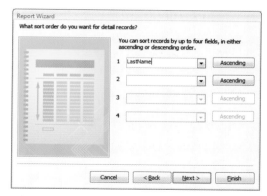

Figure 7-8
Choose a field by which to sort, if desired.

5. The default is ascending order (A to Z); if you want Descending, click the Ascending button to toggle it to read Descending.

6. If you want further levels of sorting, set them up in the 2 through 4 drop-down lists. Then click Next.

7. Select a layout for the report. See the sample area to the left of the buttons for a preview of the selected layout. See Figure 7-9.

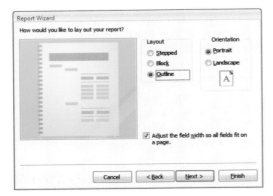

Figure 7-9
Select a layout and page orientation.

The available layouts depend on whether or not you chose to do any grouping. If you did not choose to do any grouping, the available layouts are Columnar, Tabular, and Justified, which were described earlier in the chapter. A columnar report is like the default form layout; a tabular report is like the default datasheet layout. A justified report is a hybrid of the two.

If you chose grouping, you can choose from Stepped, Block, or Outline. The main difference between Stepped, Block, and Outline is where the headings are placed.

8. Choose Portrait or Landscape to determine the page orientation of the report.

9. (Optional) Mark or clear the Adjust the Field Width So All Fields Fit on a Page check box. When this check box is marked, Access makes the report a single page wide, even if it has to decrease the widths of each column to the point where the content is truncated. Then click Next.

> If your report contains more than five or six fields, consider using Landscape orientation because it provides more breathing room for the field widths.

10. Select the formatting style you want. See the sample area to the left of the list for a preview of the selected style. See Figure 7-10. Then click Next.

> You can change the formatting style of the report later, in Layout or Design view, so do not worry too much about choosing the perfect style as you are completing the wizard.

Figure 7-10
Select a formatting style for the report.

11. Type a title for the report.

12. Click Finish. The report appears in Print Preview.

13. Click Close Print Preview.

The reason step 13 is there—closing Print Preview —is that as long as you are in Print Preview, none of the other tabs or controls are available. All you have to work with is the Print Preview tab. You'll learn how to work in Print Preview later in this chapter.

Creating a Report in Layout View

To start a new blank report in Layout view and add exactly the fields and content you want to it, choose Create > Reports > Blank Report. A blank grid appears, along with the Field List task pane. As you can see in Figure 7-11, by default there are no tables visible in the Field List pane.

Figure 7-12
Drag a field from the Field List pane to the layout.

Figure 7-11
Start a new blank report in Layout view.

To add fields to the report, follow these steps:

1. If needed, click Show All Tables in the Field List task pane. A list of all the tables in the database appears, with a plus sign next to each table name.

2. Click the plus sign next to the desired table to expand its field list.

3. Click a field to select it, and then drag it onto the report layout. It appears as a column there, with all the records from the data source previewed. See Figure 7-12.

4. Repeat step 3 to add more fields from that table.

> As you drag a field onto the layout, a vertical line appears showing where the field will go. To place a field between two existing fields, position the mouse pointer between the two fields so that the vertical line appears there, and then release the mouse button to drop the field in that spot. The field to the right moves over to make room for it.

5. (Optional) If you need to select fields from another table, click the plus sign next to another table's name in the Fields Available in Other Tables area of the Field List task pane, and then repeat step 3 as needed.

Creating a new report in Design view is somewhat labor-intensive because many of the automated layout features in Layout view are not available, such as automatically placing field labels in the Page Header section. Therefore, it is usually better to create the report in Layout view, and then fine-tune it in Design view. If you want to try your hand at a new report in Design view, choose Create > Reports > Report Design, and then drag fields into the Detail area, the same as you did to drag fields onto a layout in Layout view.

Distributing a Report

YOU WILL PROBABLY WANT TO do some additional work on your report before distributing it, such as tweaking its formatting or adding special features like aggregate totals. But before we get into those advanced features, let's take a quick foray into how to view and distribute a report.

Working with Print Preview

Print Preview, like Print Preview in other Microsoft Office applications, lets you see exactly how the report will look when printed. It also contains buttons on its tab that control page setup options like margins and page orientation.

In Print Preview, the mouse pointer appears as a magnifying glass when it is over the report. You can click anywhere in the report to toggle between a view of the whole report and the most recent zoom value. You can set the zoom value by choosing Print Preview > Zoom > Zoom. (Click the down arrow at the bottom of the button, not the button face.) See Figure 7-13.

Printing a Report

You can print a report from Print Preview by choosing Print Preview > Print > Print. This opens the Print dialog box; from there you can choose a different printer, number of copies, and print range if desired. See Figure 7-14. Then click OK.

You can also print the report from other views as well. To print from any view, choose Office > Print > Print.

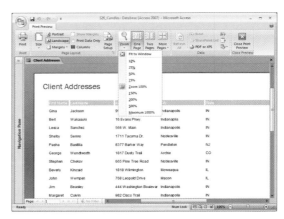

Figure 7-13
Set the zoom level for Print Preview.

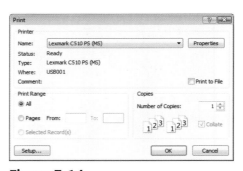

Figure 7-14
Print the report.

Distributing a Report via E-Mail

Distributing the report via e-mail saves paper and provides the recipient with a copy of the report that they (arguably) can't misplace as easily. To send the report via e-mail, follow these steps:

1. With the report open (any view), choose Office > E-mail. The Send Object As dialog box opens. See Figure 7-15.

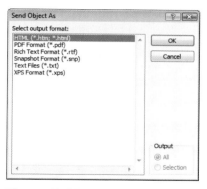

Figure 7-15
Choose the format for sending the report in an e-mail.

2. Select the desired format and click OK. Table 7-1 describes each of the formats and discusses their pros and cons.

3. If you choose HTML, an HTML Output Options dialog box appears. From here you can select an HTML Template (advanced, not covered in this chapter), and choose a type of text encoding (stick with the Default Encoding option unless you have a reason to use Unicode or Unicode [UTF-8].)

4. A new e-mail appears in your default e-mail application, with the report file as an attachment. Compose and send the e-mail as you normally would.

Table 7-1 Formats for Sending a Report in E-Mail

HTML	Standard Web page coding; generates an .html file as an e-mail attachment. **Pros:** Displays without a converter or helper program in almost all e-mail programs. **Cons:** Report layout and formatting may change somewhat.
PDF Format	Adobe Acrobat format, a popular page description language. Generates a .pdf file as an e-mail attachment. **Pros:** Report looks exactly as it does onscreen in Access. **Cons:** Requires recipient to have Adobe Acrobat Reader (free from www.adobe.com) or some other application or add-in that reads PDF files. To save in this format, you may need to download an add-in for Access as well.
Rich Text Format	Standard generic word processing format. Generates an .rtf file as an e-mail attachment. **Pros:** Almost all computers have a program that reads this format. All Windows-based PCs include WordPad, for example, which reads this format, and so does Microsoft Word. **Cons:** Report layout and formatting may change somewhat.
Snapshot Format	Format of Microsoft Access Snapshot Viewer. Generates an .snp file as an e-mail attachment. Snapshot Viewer is an optional free download from Microsoft. It enables people who do not have Access to view Access reports. **Pros:** Report appears exactly as it does in Access. **Cons:** Users will have to download and install Snapshot Viewer for Microsoft Access from www.microsoft.com.
Text Files	Plain text file; generates a .txt file as an e-mail attachment. **Pros:** Any computer can read this format, even the oldest and most odd computer out there. All that's required is a text editor, such as Notepad. **Cons:** You lose nearly all the formatting.
XPS Format	Microsoft XPS format, a competitor to Adobe's PDF format. Generates an .xps file as an e-mail attachment. **Pros:** Report appears exactly as it does in Access; all Windows Vista PCs have an XPS reader built into them. **Cons:** People who do not have Windows Vista will need to download an XPS reader application from www.microsoft.com. You might also need to download an add-in for Access to save in this format.

Using Report Design View

REPORT DESIGN VIEW ENABLES you to control and fine-tune each section of a report individually and precisely. It is very similar to Form Design view. Report Design view consists of a grid on which you can add, remove, resize, and reposition controls (fields, labels, and so on).

Unlike in Layout view, Report Design view does not precisely reflect the finished look of the report. That's because it contains single place-holders that represent multiple records in the Detail section. When you preview and print the report, those single placeholders will be filled in with many records. Figure 7-16 shows a report in Design view.

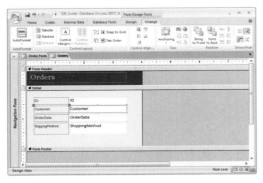

Figure 7-16
Using Report Design view

> Figure 7-16 shows Design view with the Field List task pane closed. To reopen it, choose **Design** > **Tools** > **Add Existing Fields**.

Working with Report Sections

Reports and forms are both divided into **sections**. Each section determines where the controls it contains will appear. Design view is the only place you can work with the sections and directly control their visibility, size, and content.

At a minimum, a report contains the following sections:

- ▶ **Report header, which contains the report's title, and optionally some sort of logo or graphic. Whatever you place in this section appears only at the top of the first page of the report.**

- ▶ **Page header, which contains information to be repeated at the top of each report page. In a tabular report, the page header usually contains the labels that identify the fields. In a stacked report, this section may be empty.**

- ▶ **Detail, which contains the values for the fields. In a stacked or justified report, the field names also usually appear in this section.**

- ▶ **Page footer, which contains information that appears at the bottom of each page of the report, such as the page number and date.**

- ▶ **Report footer, which contains information that appears only on the last page of the report, such as a summary statistic.**

A report also contains sections for any groupings you have created. You will learn more about managing groups later in this chapter.

Resizing a Section

To change a section's size, first move, delete, or resize any controls if you want to make the section smaller. A section cannot be resized such that the controls in it don't fit anymore. Then move the mouse pointer to the bottom edge of the section. If it is not the lowermost section, the bottom edge of the section is the top edge of the bar containing the name of the next one. For example, the bottom of the Page Header section is the top of the Detail section. When the mouse pointer becomes a double-headed vertical arrow, drag the pointer up or down to resize the section. See Figure 7-17.

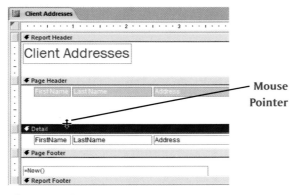

Mouse Pointer

Figure 7-17
Resizing a report section

Turning Off or Hiding Sections

If you turn off a section, any content in it is deleted. If you turn it back on, the section reappears, but it is blank, and you must reinsert controls into it. There are buttons on the Arrange tab to turn off the report and page headers and footers. See Figure 7-18. Notice that the header/footer combinations work as a team; you must turn on/off both at once. (However, you can hide one or the other, which I'll show you shortly.)

Report Header/Footer

Page Header/Footer

Figure 7-18
Turning on/off the Report Header/Footer and Page Header/Footer

If you want to turn off only one or the other (that is, only the header or only the footer), or if you want to temporarily hide one or the other without deleting its content, you can use the section's Property Sheet, as follows:

1. Click the bar for the section you want to hide.

2. Choose Design > Tools > Property Sheet. The Property Sheet task pane for that section appears.

3. In the task pane, click the Format tab, and then open the Visible property's drop-down list and choose No. See Figure 7-19.

If you hide the Detail section in a report that has groups with summary statistics (explained later in this chapter), only the group header and footer with the summaries appear. This is how you would create a summary report.

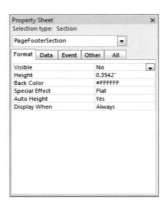

Figure 7-19
Hide a section by setting its Visible property to No.

Sorting and Grouping Data in a Report

I F YOU CREATED THE REPORT with the Report Wizard, you had the opportunity to set up sorting and grouping. If you didn't take advantage of that but now want either one, you can still add them in Design view or Layout view.

First, choose Design > Grouping & Totals > Group & Sort (if you are in Design view) or Format > Grouping & Totals > Group & Sort (if you are in Layout view). This opens a Group, Sort, and Total pane below the report. See Figure 7-20.

Figure 7-20
Use the Group, Sort, and Total pane to set up sorting and grouping.

When you create a group, the report becomes organized by that field. For example, if you group by City, each city name becomes a heading in the report, and the records appear beneath that heading for each city.

The Group, Sort, and Total pane (refer to Figure 7-20) starts out with two large buttons: Add a Group and Add a Sort. If the report already has a group or a sort applied to it, those specs appear in the pane, with each one represented by a bar. (You'll see that shortly.)

When you create a group, you can optionally also sort within it, so if you want both grouping and sorting, go with grouping.

To create a group for a report, follow these steps:

1. In the Group, Sort, and Total pane, click Add a Group. A Select Field list appears. See Figure 7-21.

2. Click the field by which to group. The report layout changes to reflect the new grouping. If you are in Layout view, notice that the group field has moved to the leftmost column. If you are in Design view, notice that the group field now has its own header and footer sections.

Figure 7-21
Select the field by which to group.

3. A grouping has a default sort order, shown in its bar in the Group, Sort, and Total pane. (For a text-based field, the default is With A on Top which is the same thing as Ascending.) If desired, click the down arrow to the right of the sort order on the grouping bar to change the order. See Figure 7-22.

Figure 7-22
Change the sort order.

4. (Optional) Click More, and then set any additional options for the grouping. For example, you can group by each unique value or a range, you can include totals or not, and you can have a group footer or not. See Figure 7-23.

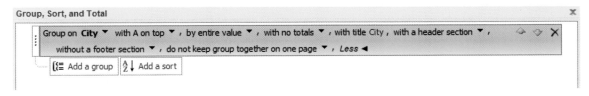

Figure 7-23
Set group options.

Sorting without grouping works the same way, except it is simpler. Click Add a Sort, and then choose the field by which to sort and a sort order, and then set any options.

Formatting a Report

NOW LET'S LOOK AT SOME ways you can format and arrange report content.

Changing the Report Layout

You can switch between Tabular and Stacked views by selecting the entire report (or the fields in the Detail section in Design view), and then choosing Arrange > Control Layout > Tabular or Arrange > Control Layout > Stacked.

The reason you select the entire report first is that Access enables you to use different layouts for different portions of the report, even down to individual fields. So you must select everything that should be in that layout before you apply it. In most cases you will want the whole report to be the same layout.

Setting Page Margins

Page margins are set on the Page Setup tab. Click the Margins button and choose one of the presets, as shown in Figure 7-24. If you have previously set custom margins, an additional choice appears on this menu: Last Custom Setting.

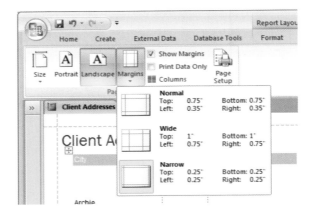

Figure 7-24
Choose a margin setting for the report printout.

Don't let the fact that the Arrange tab has a Control Margins button confuse you. The word "control" there is a noun, not a verb. That button is referring to the margins for an individual control on the form.

If you need precise margin settings that are different from any of the presets, you can use the Page Setup dialog box. Follow these steps:

1. Choose Page Setup > Page Layout > Page Setup. The Page Setup dialog box opens.

2. Click the Print Options tab.

3. Enter precise margin measurements in the Top, Bottom, Left, and Right text boxes. See Figure 7-25.

4. Click OK.

Figure 7-25
Choose a margin setting for the report printout.

> **You can manually insert your own function codes in the report in Design view. Create a new text box in Design view (Design > Controls > Text Box), and then type the function in the box, beginning with an equals sign (=).**

Formatting Individual Controls

Each individual control can be formatted individually, with text formatting such as font, font size, font attributes, horizontal alignment, font color, background color, and so on. These work just like in any other Office program (and just like when formatting a form, which you learned how to do in Chapter 3). The controls for these adjustments are found on the Format tab, in the Font group. You can also use the nearly duplicate set of font controls on the Home tab if you prefer.

When you're working in Layout view, each field appears in a box. You can set the inner and outer spacing around that box from the Arrange tab (Control Layout group):

▶ **Control Margins:** Specifies the amount of space outside the control (that is, between one control and another)

▶ **Control Padding:** Specifies the amount of space inside the control (that is, between the edge of the control's border and the text inside it)

Your choices for each of those are None, Narrow, Medium, and Wide. See Figure 7-26.

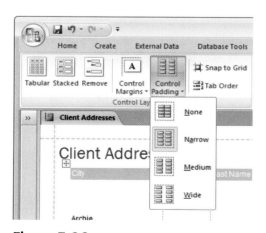

Figure 7-26
Format individual controls' padding and margins.

Adding Aggregate Functions (Totals) to a Report

YOU CAN EASILY ADD TOTALS to your reports, just like the kind you learned to put in queries in Chapter 6. Furthermore, these totals can apply to the entire report as a whole or to each group individually.

Applying Totals to a Group

To apply a total to a group, follow these steps:

1. Set up the grouping as you learned earlier in the chapter.

2. Switch to Layout view if you are not already there.

3. If the Group, Sort, and Total pane does not already appear, choose Format > Grouping & Totals > Group & Sort to display it.

4. On the bar for the group specification, click More to display the full set of options if they do not already appear.

5. Click the down arrow to the right of With No Totals to open a menu of aggregate functions. See Figure 7-27.

Figure 7-27
Choose a total function to appear for each group.

6. Choose the field on which to perform the total. It need not be the same as the field by which you are grouping.

7. Choose the type of function you want from the Type list.

8. Mark the check boxes for Show Grand Total and/or Show Group Totals as % of Grand Total if desired.

9. Mark either the Show in Group Header or Show in Group Footer check box (or both) to indicate where the total should appear.

10. Click away from the menu to close it.

Applying Totals to the Entire Report

Some totals should apply to the entire report, not to each specific group. For this type of total, follow these steps to insert the appropriate code:

1. In Layout view, select the column heading label for the field to which you want to apply an aggregate function.

2. Choose Format > Grouping & Totals > Totals. A menu appears showing the available functions for that field.

> **For a text field, only Count Records and Count Values are available.**

3. Click the desired function. It is inserted as a code at the bottom of the report.

To see the code that you inserted, switch to Design view and look in the Report Footer area. It appears in its own box. For example, if you chose Count Records, you will see =Count(*) there.

Index